Ken Burns's

THE CIVIL WAR

HISTORIANS RESPOND

edited by

Robert Brent Toplin

New York   Oxford

OXFORD UNIVERSITY PRESS

1996

Oxford University Press

Oxford   New York
Athens   Auckland   Bangkok   Bombay
Calcutta   Cape Town   Dar es Salaam   Delhi
Florence   Hong Kong   Istanbul   Karachi
Kuala Lumpur   Madras   Madrid   Melbourne
Mexico City   Nairobi   Paris   Singapore
Taipei   Tokyo   Toronto
and associated companies in
Berlin   Ibadan

Copyright © 1996 by Robert Brent Toplin

Published by Oxford University Press, Inc.,
198 Madison Avenue, New York, New York 10016

Oxford is a registered trademark of Oxford University Press

Library of Congress Cataloging-in-Publication Data

Ken Burns's *The Civil War* : historians respond/
edited by Robert Brent Toplin.
p. cm.   Includes bibliographical references.
ISBN 0-19-509330-5
1. Civil War (Television program)   2. United States—History—
Civil War, 1861–1865—Motion pictures and the war.   I. Toplin,
Robert Brent, 1940–
E468.9.K46   1996
973.7—dc20   95-12190

987654321

Printed in the United States of America
on acid-free paper

Preface

The idea for this book emerged in 1993 when I witnessed two
lively disagreements among historians concerning Ken Burns's
The Civil War. The first experience occurred at a three-day
conference on history and film sponsored by the New England
Foundation for the Humanities. More than 800 people had
gathered at the meetings, many of them because Ken Burns
had been scheduled as a speaker and his documentary *The
Civil War* identified as the principal subject for discussion
during the first day. Enthusiasm for Burns's achievement ran
high. People in the audience wanted to know more about the
making of Burns's documentary, and they hoped to learn how
his techniques could be applied to other film projects. As
events unfolded, the audience also learned how *The Civil War*
could arouse controversy. In the first session two scholars,
Leon Litwack and Daniel Walkowitz, offered sharply critical

comments on Burns's presentation of history. Litwack's and Walkowitz's remarks provoked animated discussions for the duration of the conference. A few months later I encountered similar arguments at a conference on history and film sponsored by the Rutgers Center for Historical Analysis. After delivering a generally positive overview of *The Civil War*, some historians disagreed strongly with my conclusions. Repeating criticisms aired at the Boston conference, they suggested that Burns could have done more in the documentary to reflect trends in modern scholarship. As in Boston, these remarks sparked a dramatic exchange of opinion. A number of historians responded by defending or attacking Burns's work.

Interestingly, the objections raised in these meetings did not constitute totally damning indictments. The critics did not suggest Burns's documentary was devoid of educational value. Instead, they participated in a sort of lovers' quarrel. Most of them appreciated Burns's skill as a master storyteller, particularly his talent for presenting history in fascinating ways and stimulating the public's interest in learning about America's past. The critics' disagreements focused particularly on the question: *Which stories* about the Civil War ought to be told and *which conclusions* should be drawn from the evidence? Some thought Burns devoted too much time to military matters. They wanted a documentary that incorporated more social history of the war years. Burns needed to provide greater insight on race, gender, and class as well as economics and politics, they charged. The documentary concentrated too much on a traditional story about generals, soldiers, and battles. There were others who disagreed with the emphases in Burns's interpretation (i.e., they pointed not to what was left out but with what was included). These critics sought greater

attention to slavery's effect on military and political developments or stressed the importance of military campaigns that
seemed to be underplayed in Burns's documentary or argued
for a different understanding of the war's overall meaning and
impact. In sum, the scholars acknowledged Burns's achievements, but they also recommended different strategies for
interpreting the lessons of the war.

After hearing these arguments and participating in them, I
concluded that a book of essays about *The Civil War* could
serve three useful purposes. First, it could expose readers to the
historians' debates. Unfortunately, the public is not very familiar with these disagreements about Burns's interpretation
of history. This book aims to take the debate outside the halls
of the academy and give it wider exposure. In jargon-free
language it provides both critical and favorable analyses of
The Civil War's portrayal of the past. Secondly, the book
provides a forum for more detailed discussion of the themes
that excited television audiences. After watching *The Civil
War*, many viewers were hungry for additional information
on the issues Burns addressed in his eleven hours of programming. It is hoped that the insights provided by several
Civil War scholars will enhance the reader's thinking about
the American experience in 1861–65. Finally, an analysis of
Burns's use of the visual media to interpret history challenges
us to ponder the promise and the limitations of film as edu-
cator. This is an important consideration in view of the
electronic media's tremendous influence in modern society.
Many citizens now get their ideas about history from film and
television as well as from books and classroom lectures. Film
and television penetrate lives, conveying messages about the
past in subtle but often powerful ways. As Burns's documen-

tary demonstrates, a well-constructed television program can teach as well as entertain. While examining scholars' reactions to *The Civil War*, then, we can ask: Is film in some ways superior to a book as a communicator of feeling and understanding? In which ways does history on film fail to match the potential of written history? How much education should we expect from a documentary such as *The Civil War*, a production that seeks both to achieve high audience ratings and please teachers and scholars?

In considering these questions we can profit by observations from the filmmakers themselves, and, fortunately, this volume contains contributions from two critically important figures. Ken Burns, *The Civil War*'s producer and director, and Geoffrey Ward, the chief writer, are among the contributors to this volume. Their involvement reflects an admirable posture of responsibility to the historical profession. Burns and Ward could easily have avoided the confrontation. Indeed, many filmmakers would do just that, not caring to face the challenge of scholars' critiques. Many producers, directors, and writers choose to remain distant from the cut and thrust of debates over interpretation. By identifying themselves as "artists" rather than as filmmaker-historians, they suggest that they have no more obligation to comment on their work than does a painter to respond to the judgments of critics. Yet Burns and Ward accepted the invitation to participate in this project without hesitation.

Burns's willingness to confront comments about his filmmaking is in keeping with the receptivity he has demonstrated over many years. More than any other producer of historical films that I am familiar with, he has participated in dialogues with the public and with professional historians through participation in conferences and in interviews with the press. Since the early 1980s, he has fielded numerous questions about his documentaries, opening himself to both friendly and hostile remarks. His willingness to debate important questions is well illustrated in a lengthy interview that appeared in the December 1994 issue of the *Journal of American History*. In that conversation Burns responded to a number of penetrating queries about his approach to historical research and interpretation from historian/editor David Thelen. In the interview Burns expounded on his personal philosophy of history, and he demonstrated readiness to lock horns with his critics and articulate his own complaints about trends in scholarship. In that interview and in various other exchanges, Burns revealed that he was not afraid to speak as a "historian" as well as a "filmmaker." Our thinking about historical documentaries would be enhanced if other filmmakers would avoid hiding behind the "artist's" shield and face pointed questions about their work as Burns has done.

All of the historians contributing to this volume have engaged in research associated with the Civil War era. C. Vann Woodward, a specialist on southern history now retired from Yale University, served as a principal adviser to Burns. He relates his experiences working on the inside of the film project. Robert Brent Toplin, editor of the volume and editor of film reviews for the *Journal of American History* and creator of a number of dramatic films on slavery and the Civil War that appeared on PBS Television and The Disney Channel, considers the influence of the present on Burns's interpretation of the war. Gary W. Gallagher, chairperson of the history department at Penn State and a specialist on military history, examines Burns's interpretation of military issues. Catherine Clinton, a historian formerly associated with Harvard University who is now participating in filmmaking, examines *The Civil War*'s treatment of women's experiences in the war. Gabor Boritt, Director of the Civil War Institute at Gettysburg and professor at Gettysburg College, examines Burns's treatment of Lincoln and the Battle of Gettysburg. Eric Foner of Columbia University, author of numerous studies concerning Civil War and Reconstruction issues, considers Burns's interpretation of the war's significance, and Leon Litwack, professor of history at the University of California at Berkeley and author of studies of the African-American experience in the Civil War and Reconstruction, expands on the critique he delivered at the conference sponsored by the New England Foundation for the Humanities.

Wilmington, N. C.   R.B.T.
March 1995

Contents

Introduction

ROBERT BRENT TOPLIN

*I*N SEPTEMBER 1990, *The Civil War* made television history. The eleven-hour series broke the PBS audience-record for an educational series (*Cosmos*, Carl Sagan's 1980 program, had been the previous leader). In many metropolitan areas it attracted more viewers than the regular entertainment fare on the major networks. An estimated 13.9 million Americans watched *The Civil War*'s first broadcast, and many more tuned into later programs (about 40 million watched one or more broadcasts). Then millions more saw subsequent broadcasts on TV, purchased videos, or viewed the series in connection with school, college, or adult education classes. Additional millions enthusiastically watched *The Civil War* when it appeared on television in Great Britain, Germany, Japan, and other nations. The series also had a spillover effect in the United States, stirring the public's hunger for knowledge about the war. In the weeks and months after broadcast, attendance at Civil War battle sites rose significantly, and books about the subject sold briskly. One author who profited from the bonanza was Shelby Foote, the historian who appeared in several of Burns's episodes. Foote told Burns the documentary turned him into "a millionaire." He had sold 30,000 copies of his war trilogy in fifteen years; during the six months after the broadcast, Foote sold more than 100,000 sets.

The Civil War's popularity brought Ken Burns an attractive overture from Disney Studios suggesting that Burns come to California and explore opportunities in commercial filmmaking. The 37-year-old filmmaker did not accept the invitation, however, choosing to remain in New Hampshire to continue production of historical documentaries. He followed *The Civil War* with *Empire of the Air: The Men Who Made Radio*, and in 1994 released *Baseball*, a film that rivaled *The Civil War* in ambition and breadth of coverage.

Ken Burns had become interested in filmmaking during his years as a student at Hampshire College, an institution whose founders aimed to foster student creativity through an innovative learning environment. In Burns's case they clearly succeeded. In Burns's last year at Hampshire he presented a sophisticated documentary as his senior thesis, a film about Old Sturbridge Village (a restored New England community). After graduation, Burns established Florentine Films with some college buddies, naming the firm after a nearby Massachusetts town where a favorite teacher lived. Burns's interest in American history was evident in the themes he chose for subsequent documentaries (interestingly, he had taken only one history course in college and that in Russian history). *Brooklyn Bridge* (1982), his first major production, garnered an Academy Award nomination and numerous awards. The production featured historian David McCullough as narrator (McCullough had written an important book on the history of the bridge's construction). This collaboration established a long-term friendship and placed McCullough as a familiar commentator in Burns's productions (including *The Civil War*). Several documentaries followed: *The Shakers: Hands to Work, Hearts to God* (1984); *Huey Long* (1985); *The Statue of Liberty* (1985); *Thomas Hart Benton* and *The Congress* (1988).

A stipulation in the grant from the National Endowment for the Humanities, which propelled initial planning for *The Civil War*, demanded collaboration between creative artists and scholars. Such cooperation was familiar to Burns (he had worked closely with historians in all of his previous documentary projects), but it led to friction in the early stages of discussions regarding *The Civil War*. Burns encountered significant resistance from some individuals attending an advisory board meeting. On one occasion when the historians gathered to review a first draft of the script, a few of them complained that the document related an old-fashioned nineteenth-century version of the Civil War story by giving too much attention to military affairs. Burns explained that the draft was a working document, that he welcomed his advisers' recommendations, and that the production team intended to make use of the advisers' suggestions in subsequent drafts. C. Vann Woodward, a participant in that meeting and defender of Burns in the heated discussions, offered a pointed response at the meeting (see Woodward's description in this book).

As the film began to take shape, PBS officials, corporate underwriters, and book publishers sensed the quality of the forthcoming production and conjectured that broadcast of

The Civil War could draw considerable viewer attention. Administrators at PBS agreed to highlight the production with an unusual format: they would run programs in the series back-to-back on consecutive nights for an entire week (ABC had been tremendously successful with similar programming strategy in the 1970s in its broadcast of the historical drama *Roots*). Publicity for *The Civil War* was essential, since not all that many Americans were in a habit of watching documentaries on PBS Television. General Motors responded handsomely to this challenge, providing $1.5 million for promotion. Furthermore, publishing executives realized that a successful TV series about the greatest tragedy in American history would be likely to stimulate spinoff sales of print materials. They agreed to pay a $375,000 advance for a lavishly illustrated book related to the series. While all of this pre-broadcast activity revealed an expectation of success, before September 1990 the major underwriters and Burns himself did not fully sense that they were dealing with a unique phenomenon: a documentary about to prove itself a blockbuster.

During the week of broadcast, the topic of the Civil War became a familiar subject of conversation in homes, schools, workplaces, bars, and commuter trains. Thousands of letters from excited fans poured into Burns's office at Florentine Films, as enthusiasts eloquently described their emotional reactions to the film and related information about their ancestors' experiences in the Civil War. Burns was an instant celebrity. He appeared on the Johnny Carson show and had to deal with hero-worshippers who mobbed him in public places.

Why did *The Civil War* make such an extraordinary impact? Why did viewer enthusiasm soar well beyond interest in hundreds of other historical documentaries that appeared on American television in previous years?

Certainly, the subject matter contributed to the success. No topic from U.S. history had excited as much curiosity from Americans and foreigners as the sectional conflict of 1861–65. The war represented the only situation in U.S. history in which Americans could not work out their differences within the political system and turned instead to killing each other under separate flags and governments. The subject also excited interest because of the carnage associated with it. More than 600,000 Americans perished in the war. Two days at the Shiloh battlefield resulted in more deaths than in all previous American wars. One day at Antietam became the bloodiest in American history. It is not surprising, then, that readers have long demonstrated curiosity about this great national tragedy.

Still, the public's hunger for information about the Civil War could not alone explain why the broadcast became an important event in the history of education-oriented television. Numerous other documentaries and docudramas dealing with themes from the Civil War era had appeared on TV, yet they did not come close to arousing the audience response that Burns's film did. Clearly, much of the success of the series related to Burns's skills as a filmmaker. The young artist had managed to present his subject in a fascinating way.

Burns demonstrated that he was an extraordinarily effective craftsman of film, and the popularity of the series may be attributed in large part to his skills as a communicator. Burns had established his own technique by 1990, a style of presenting history on television that became his own artistic signature. Other filmmakers employed aspects of his method, but Burns developed a reputation for orchestrating these technical elements with particular elegance and sophistication. One hallmark of his work concerned the rejection of fictional elements and concentration on authentic evidence from the past.

In making *The Civil War*, for example, Burns did not incorporate re-enactments by modern-day figures dressed as soldiers or feature actors in period costumes or draw upon dramatic excerpts from Hollywood movies. Instead, he focused on authentic sources from the war—photographs, lithographs, paintings, newspapers, letters, signs, handbills, and other items. His handling of photographs was masterful, for the primitive photography of the 1860s required that subjects stand still and pose (cameras had not been fast enough then to capture movement effectively). *The Civil War* injected life in these visual documents, nonetheless, by examining them as an art historian would scan a painting. With considerable sensitivity, the camera read messages from the pictures, focusing on specific elements of the images while words, sounds, and music provided accent. Burns's camera also took the viewer to the modern-day locales of the battlefields, using present-day cinematography to show the sites where tragedy had occurred in the 1860s. Sometimes the camera rushed across a ridge or weaved between trees in the woods, giving audiences a feeling for the terror soldiers experienced as they dodged unseen enemies. At other moments Burns quietly studied a windy field while the film encouraged viewers to ponder life in a distant time in history. Interestingly, Burns often succeeded in stirring the viewer's imagination while showing modern-day physical settings devoid of human figures.

The mystery of this achievement becomes less baffling when we recognize that *The Civil War* offered its audiences much more than just a visual experience. A great deal of the film's communication came through the medium of sound. Ambient noise of horses' galloping, cannons' firing, and men screaming punctuated the story while the camera concentrated on photos or present-day battle sites. Music also carried messages and contributed to the sense of authenticity. Throughout the series, audiences heard the tunes that moved soldiers and citizens of the war era, such as "Battle Hymn of the Republic," "Rally Round the Flag, Boys," and "Dixie." One of the most memorable melodies, a refrain with a haunting suggestion of life in the nineteenth century, was actually created in the late twentieth century. Composer Jay Ungar wrote "Ashokan Farewell," the remarkable piece that served as the principal musical theme for *The Civil War*.

Words were also essential in the documentary. Burns presented much of his story in the language of the people who lived through the wartime experience. He had begun experimenting with these "quotations" as a young filmmaker in college, and, through the years, Burns has given them prominent places in his films. *The Civil War* incorporated over 900 quotations. Many were familiar to readers of books about the war, such as Lincoln's observation, "If there's a worse place than hell, I'm in it," and an African-American's comment during the war when his fortunes improved: "Hello, massa. Bottom rail on top this time." Numerous other quotations from the era were less well known, and their appearance in the film reflected the successful research efforts of Burns and his fellow researchers. One of the interesting discoveries concerned the diary of Elisha Hunt Rhodes, which Burns had bought from a fellow townsman after finding it in an antique shop. Burns considered the Rhodes diary wonderfully evocative of the thoughts of a Union soldier, and he gave Rhodes's observations a prominent place in the film.

Technical artistry was critical to Burns's success in making history appealing, but there was another essential element that was psychological rather than technical. Burns managed to help viewers *feel* the experience of war.

When speaking about his efforts to produce *The Civil War*, Ken Burns called himself "a historian of emotions." Emotion "is the great glue of history," he said, the cement that makes the meaning of facts stick in viewers' minds. Film not only presents information; it sharpens the audience's sense of the importance of the facts. It "has the power to reach profound levels of emotion," Burns pointed out, "and I can't be interested in a piece of history unless there's something I can loosely describe as emotional about it. I think the ordinary person feels that way too." Burns argued that film is not primarily about dates and facts. "It is *all* about people and their passions."

A good illustration of Burns's attention to the emotional dimension of history can be seen toward the end of the first program. In that segment audiences heard a reading of the now-famous letter Sullivan Ballou wrote to his wife shortly before he died in the first battle at Bull Run. Ballou's words appeared against a background of beautiful cinematography showing the fields where the Yankee figure fell. This moment in the film brought many viewers to tears. It evoked sensitivity to the tragedy at Bull Run more effectively than narration or visual presentations could.

Several of the program's most memorable emotion-laden moments occurred toward the end of the series. The presentation of Lincoln's visit to the Confederate capital of Richmond in the last days of the war, particularly the treatment of Lincoln's decision to sit at the desk of the Confederate leader Jefferson Davis, was emotionally powerful. So was the portrayal of Robert E. Lee's surrender to Ulysses S. Grant at Appomatox. Even more memorable was the presentation of John Wilkes Booth's assassination of Lincoln at Ford's Theatre. Burns secured the services of a Washington acting team for a reading of the play, *Our American Cousin*, which the President witnessed on his last night. As television viewers heard words from the Victorian comedy and saw the interior of Ford's Theatre, they encountered painful hints of the tragedy about to unfold. Burns's technique drew the viewers' emotions into the historical scene, giving them the impression of being present in the past.

The achievement in arousing feeling for history was particularly encouraging to educators, because Burns delivered this stimulus through the medium of television. TV had received much criticism since the 1950s for failing to live up to the promise that its early enthusiasts suggested (many had thought it would prove a tremendous instrument for education). Critics complained about television's presentation of the lowest common denominator in entertainment, observing the prominence of crime and comic drama on TV and the relative scarcity of sophisticated, mind-stimulating programming. Many concluded that entertainment and education could not mix well in American-style television, and they looked to books as far better sources of understanding. The success of *The Civil War* seemed to challenge this negative conclusion. It appeared to demonstrate that television had the potential to entertain and educate at the same time.

While Burns accomplished a great deal through television, it is important to recognize, too, that his filmed perspective on history did not present a full account of the Civil War experience. Many elements in the story were absent in his documentary or received only limited attention. To identify what was missing or got brief consideration is not necessarily to criticize the filmmaker. No television documentary can be expected to provide a truly comprehensive treatment of a historical subject. There are not enough broadcast hours to "cover" all relevant subjects adequately. A script of the words spoken in an hour-long documentary may amount to no more than a dozen to twenty pages—a relatively small information load. Film "is not equipped to do what a book does," admits Burns, "which is to attain profound levels of meaning and texture." Burns sees film as a stimulus to interest. A television program can excite the viewers' curiosity, he says, and stir them to seek depth of knowledge through further reading.

While film is an attractive medium for showing dramatic confrontations and violent action, it is often less successful in communicating concepts or exploring ideas in depth. Film can effectively relate the personal side of the past, introducing audiences to individuals from history, but it is often disappointing when analyzing broad trends. Both in documentaries and docudramas, filmmakers usually concentrate on personalities and their impact on history, giving much less attention to impersonal forces. Filmmakers know, for instance, that broad economic changes often make a profound impact on people's lives. They sense, however, that reporting on such a topic does not tend to involve audiences. Filmmakers realize that their productions are more likely to prove appealing if they concentrate on telling interesting stories about the way specific people effected change through the force of individual personalities and actions.

We can regret the absence of a more thorough discussion of impersonal factors, but in wishing for greater comprehensiveness we should not lose sight of the distinctive character of history on film. It is not the same as history on the printed page. If filmmakers try to touch every popular issue briefly, they are likely to confuse or bore their audiences. Rather than attempt to present a visual encyclopedia, documentarists usually focus on particular subjects. They give attention to the highly dramatic elements in history. Filmmakers understand, for example, that scenes of tension and conflict are likely to attract audience interest. It is not surprising, then, that Burns's compelling documentary concentrated on war themes, subjects that work well for TV.

Evidence of this pattern can be seen in the emphasis of the series on the story of generals, soldiers, and battles. Burns devoted much less study to the home front and to subjects such as industrialization, finance, inflation, and the draft. Issues regarding dissent during wartime received scant attention as did decisions by the Supreme Court. These subjects were addressed, to be sure, but to a lesser degree. Also, the important topic of foreign policy received minor attention, especially the significant subject of the Confederacy's attempts to gain recognition from France and from Great Britain. Women made appearances throughout the programs by way of the quotations from Mary Boykin Chesnut and reports on the wartime activities of Clara Barton and Dorothea Dix. Their cameos were "politically correct" for 1990, but the series did not move far beyond mini-biographies and general remarks. Some aspects of the fighting also received only brief attention. For instance, after presenting a graphic description of the battle between the *Monitor* and the *Merrimack*, relatively little else was said about naval warfare. Only a little was reported on the important Union blockade of Confederate ports, the role of southern blockade runners, or the significance of ironclads after the *Monitor-Merrimack* confrontation.

While examining the contributors' assessments of Burns's treatment of history, readers ought to consider some of the fundamental questions about interpreting history on film that these observations suggest. As mentioned above, for example, the documentary presents some aspects of the Civil War in colorful detail while giving only limited attention to other elements. Is this selectiveness justified? Would the film have been better had Burns given more time to the issues of interest to the authors in this book? Does the absence of greater attention to the suggested subjects reflect significant problems in the film's perspective on the Civil War? Or, do the critics expect too much? Shouldn't Burns have the right to interpret the war in terms of the issues he considers important? Can we appreciate the artist's interest in concentrating on stories that appear to work well on film and leave for books the subjects that work less well for the visual medium? Indeed, shouldn't Burns's critics recognize that no single documentary can provide a completely comprehensive picture of the war? If there are gaps in the film under study, is not the appropriate remedy to seek production of *other* films about the war years that accent *other* perspectives rather than to demand a different product from Burns?

If the opinions registered in this book are highly judgmental, it is because scholars believe that the stakes are very high. *The Civil War* is no ordinary documentary. It aroused interest in history as no other recent educational film has. The extraordinary reception demonstrated that a single television series could stimulate millions of people in the United States and the world to think seriously about the experiences of the past. In short, debates about *The Civil War* became intense, because the documentary represented perhaps the best modern American example of film's potential to teach history on a mass scale. In holding Burns's production to high scholarly standards, then, the contributors have acknowledged the significance of his accomplishment.

Ken Burns's

THE CIVIL WAR

1

Help From Historians

C. Vann Woodward

*I*T IS LIKELY THAT FROM the time artists began to use, portray, or celebrate historical subjects their freedom to invent, to imagine, and to alter as against their obligations to accuracy, to fact, and to "truth" has been debated. Were artists makers of myth, or were they seekers of truth? Were they to tell it like it should have been or like it really had been? Opinion was divided on all these questions, even among artists themselves, for they can be found on both sides of the ongoing debate. The jury is still out on the question, and the debate continues.

I had learned from advising him in the production of *Huey Long*, a TV film about the Louisiana politician, on which side Ken Burns took his stand. For him the real and true were dramatic enough, and he was at pains first of all to get the story straight and to make up nothing. My brief experience with the *Huey Long* production confirmed impressions derived from seeing earlier works of Burns, such as *The Statue of Liberty* and *Brooklyn Bridge*. Later on, in conversation and correspondence and in some speeches of his, I found many attitudes, opinions, and convictions that historians find congenial and that I share myself.

For Burns there were no easy solutions to problems raised by contradictions between authorities and conflicting evidence. He would prefer to let both sides have their say. Nor should there be any foregone conclusions, any commitment to prove something, or any evasion of hard questions, but rather a constant search for answers. While he readily admitted that his vocation was "not precisely the same as the historians'," he nevertheless believed that "it shared many of the aims and much of the spirit." If the historian delights in "telling us what our history is and what it means," the maker of films "as often delights in recording and conveying the simple fact that we had a history at all: that there was once a time when people looked like this, or sounded like that, or felt these ways about such things."[1]

As for the tensions between art and science, he would strive to strike a balance between such polarities, as he believed all good history did. In the face-off between "top-down" and "bottom-up" historians, Ken and his brother Ric Burns tended to lean toward the latter camp in their Civil War series. After all, their great-great-grandfather Abraham Burns, a Confederate cavalryman, was a blacksmith in civilian life. The lowly, the common people, the unsung and forgotten were fully represented. But the famous and the powerful, the generals and the presidents, were by no means neglected. The poetry of Lincoln's greatest addresses provides much of the background music for the series. At the beginning of the project Ken Burns asked me to name a book or two that he "should begin to read to understand the Civil War." He later expressed special gratitude for my suggesting *John Brown's Body* by the poet Stephen Vincent Bénet as a good "place to start." Recalling this episode later, Burns described the series as being "like a poem—selective, impressionistic, to be sure, but a legitimate form of historic expression."[2]

So it was that when Burns asked me in 1985 to be a consultant in his Civil War project, I had little hesitation in accepting his invitation. At that time I had no idea the work would run on for five years, and I doubt that Ken and Ric did either. Much of the consultation was carried on by informal conversation about books, sources, and personalities. One of my first contributions was helping to suggest members of the panel of consultants, twenty-four in all, mainly but not entirely historians. I was glad to see two non-academic historians, Shelby Foote and David McCullough, already on board.

My suggestions were mainly academics, including some of my former students, two of them Pulitzer Prize winners, and all intensely engaged in Civil War history writing. Jim McPherson was completing his superb volume *Battle Cry of Freedom*; Bill McFeely had recently published his splendid *Grant* and was at work on Douglass; Barbara Fields had just brought out her fine book on slavery in Maryland. My old friend, Robert Penn Warren, then in his last years, added greatly to the distinction of the panel.

Other members had devoted more of their careers to the Civil War than I had and achieved much greater distinction in their work on the subject. In some ways, however, I felt closer to the period. For one thing, with the exception of Warren, I was the oldest one of the group and, in the literal sense, that much closer to the period. More important was the closeness derived from growing up in the South when The War was still a very live subject of conversation. At my grandmother's dinner table I sat as a child with veterans of the defeated army, including my grandfather, discharged at the age of nineteen after four years' service in the ranks. Down the road from the house but within sight was the cottage of a former slave, whose wife often came to visit my grandmother on a Saturday afternoon.

The first assignment of the panel was to comment on the draft prepared to support an application for a grant from the National Endowment for the Humanities. I quote the opening paragraph of my comment on the draft:

> I was much taken with your draft of the Civil War Project— the way it avoids the didactic and the pedantic, the way it brings together the image and the word, the event and the moral; the way it captures the drama and escapes the tedium of history; the happy counterpointing of opposite numbers, paradoxes, contrasts, and counterparts. It is an exciting way of working with history.[3]

I went on to offer a number of criticisms, point out errors, and make some suggestions. The response to my letter came from Ric Burns who, after thanking me, writes:

> We have, I believe it's correct to say, incorporated all of your criticisms into the final version of the proposal, and are pleased to have had your guidance in time to avoid a number of embarrassing gaffes (Jefferson Davis no longer wears women's clothes [when captured] in our treatment).[4]

It is not meant to suggest that the panel of consultants did more than offer comment and criticism at various stages and successive drafts of work in progress. That work was done by the Burns brothers and their staff, including five editors, four researchers, more than eighty archivists of museums and libraries, and scores of others, including two helicopter pilots and all those cameramen filming 16,000 photographs, paintings, and broadsides. The consulting went on collectively as well as individually.

On the individual plane there were both phone calls and visits. The Burns brothers paid me a visit at my home in Hamden, Connecticut. They were especially interested in a recent work of mine, the huge *Mary Chesnut's Civil War*, and wanted me to select "passages appropriate to each section of the film," many of which they used as running comments on events in the final version. Professional actors were persuaded to read (for free!) passages from wartime characters frequently quoted, and I was fortunate enough to have Julie Harris, one of my favorite screen stars, read the Chesnut passages and do it beautifully.[5]

Two members of our group were singled out to perform in person in the film. These were Shelby Foote and Barbara Fields, both speaking their own minds without script. Both of them proved to be endowed with natural and unsuspected gifts as cinematic performers. Many viewers thought them stars of the film. I was experimentally and earnestly photographed by Ken himself with such a role in mind; but for some mysterious reason, possibly photogenic, I was deprived of TV fame, or more probably of future embarrassment, and do not regret the deprivation. At least I am not stopped in the street by unknown autograph seekers.

Two years and more into the shooting, cutting, revising, and reviewing of the TV film, a book version of the Civil War show was proposed by an editor at Alfred A. Knopf as the companion volume to the TV series. With a narrative by Geoffrey C. Ward based on the documentary filmscript by Ward, Ric Burns, and Ken Burns, it was to have in addition five essays, one for each of the five sections of the book. I agreed to write the final essay under the title "What the War Made Us," after Ric Burns's avowal that "we can't really envision the book without you." The essays were to be "thematic pieces, essentially, not narrative ones."[6] Whatever the merits of the essays and the excerpts from the film script, the primary appeal of the gorgeous resulting volume was probably the more than 500 illustrations, including rare Civil War photographs, many never before published.

Which reminds me to mention the fact that this was the first war in all history to be extensively photographed while in progress. The photographers of the time had already developed considerable skill and were to gain more of it from their wartime experience. Without the riches of their work the TV series would have lacked one vital source of its appeal and one secret of its success.

But back to the making. The makers seemed grateful for the periodic assessment of their work in progress by the historians and scholars making up the panel of consultants, eager for their reaction and reassured by their approval. Ken Burns certainly shared these feelings. But he wanted to be sure, however, that all sides and points of view were represented, for he knew that historians were not of one mind and spent much time debating their differences. Was I sure that some schools and points of view were not being overlooked?

What about the younger generation, the dissidents, the radicals? I promised to think it over. I then arranged for him to show extensive excerpts from the work in progress before a group of the more able dissenters from received opinion among the younger generation. This in the absence of their elders, myself excepted.

I watched closely the reactions on both sides, those of the viewers to the film as well as those of the producers to reactions of their audience. There were some tense moments during the long afternoon. The invited viewers lost little time in moving into their posture of dissenters and critics. The film, they felt strongly, was too "neutral," too neglectful of the common soldiers, the women's role, the plain people, the slaves, and the issue of slavery and emancipation. Also it was too indulgent of leaders and heroes, to their blunders and mistakes, their cynicism, their huge casualty lists, their use of military means for political ends.

As I listened in silence I could see the growing distress of Ken and Ric Burns in their faces as well as in their desperate efforts to defend themselves and their film against such aggressive criticism. Finally I broke in with what I am afraid became something of a sermon to the critics. They should realize, I admonished, that they were not addressing their usual opponents, an older generation of historians grown complacent and out of touch with new ideas and demands. They were speaking to artists, artists whose purpose was to bring to life for the present a profound national ordeal of the past, a great tragedy as it was seen, heard, felt, lamented, and mourned, or greeted as liberation by the people who went through it in the 1860s. The artists could not be expected to abandon their true role and take sides in current generational or ideological disputes among scholars. Nor should they be required to use their art to promote political, social, or moral causes and movements of the present day, however worthy they may be. Historians should be able to help artists without attempting to use them for ends quite foreign to their art.

Thus sayeth the preacher. His sermon was followed by a prolonged silence on the part of the small congregation, and a feeling on his part of shock and surprise at his uncharacteristic outburst after years of encouraging students to question the conventional and challenge the unchallengeable. But the faces of Ken and Ric wore expressions of utmost relief. Nothing else I did for them seemed to evoke such gratitude as they later voiced for this intervention. "We will always cherish the memory of your generous and firm defense of our storytelling mandate in the face of possible pedagogical interference," wrote Ken with his own generosity three years later. "You singlehandedly turned skeptics and narrow critics into at least calmer contributors to our wildly overblown ambitions." He exaggerated the "singlehanded" aspect in extending it to the general sessions, when I had much help.

My account of dissent from a minority of critics is by no means intended to imply consensus on the part of the majority. They also had their doubts about the film and their differences with one another. These came out in the periodic meetings of the consulting panel in New York over three years to view showings at various stages of the progress of the film-making and cutting. Some of these sessions went on for two days and more, with attendance varying in number. Differences between historians continued, but with the tacit acknowledgment that some of these were old chestnuts that would be with us forever. There *was* progress, however, in advancing toward favorable consensus regarding the film itself—the real business at hand. That is, a growing feeling of confidence in the integrity and the power of the series and its makers in spite of our continued demand for improvements and corrections.

Our last full session of screening and discussion came in October of 1988 and lasted three days. The film of eleven hours in nine sections was near its final form and this was the last opportunity for revision and correction. It soon became evident as the screening went forward that the assembled critics were this time more absorbed in their appreciation than in making critical points. It was a remarkable sight—the rapt attention of these seasoned scholars, some of them strongly moved. On returning home I wrote Ken:

> In our three days of refighting the Civil War in New York last week we all doubtless suffered a bit of battle fatigue. One result, I suspect, was that in our concentration on seeking improvements, pointing out flaws, and picking nits we neglected to mention an underlying consensus. I heard it often between the lines in talk with my colleagues, but mainly it remained an unspoken assumption.[8]

My hunch was borne out in letters to Burns from my colleagues expressing much the same perception. One came from Don E. Fehrenbacher, a gifted Lincoln scholar from Stanford University, who wrote that he was "very happy about the film," and added:

> You are achieving a superior double blend of words and pictures, of scholarship and entertainment . . . What

impresses me most of all is your commitment, and that of your associates, to the achievement of excellence. I am proud to be associated with this enterprise.[9]

And from Shelby Foote came high praise and admiration:

I was pleased with practically everything I saw in the rough-cut runs of the series parts. We are truly out of the woods now; all we have to do from here on is trim some bushes and smooth some paths—which means, of course, that it's entirely in your hands from here to the finish, and I'm feeling all the way confident because the things you have to do are absolutely the things you do best . . . I feel quite good about the whole project.[10]

Bill McFeely wondered if he "had ever worked so hard in two-and-a-half days" because "all those hours of film required an enormous amount of concentration." He continued:

Having spent ten years of my life struggling with one aspect of the Civil War and being highly critical of so much of the flag-waving and drum-beating [on TV] . . . I find myself deeply in your debt for creating so strong a study of the whole war . . . and I am proud to have been a consultant and to try to lend a hand.[11]

Before seeing these letters from others I had written Burns about what I perceived then as an "unspoken assumption" among them:

That was a feeling of assurance that we were working with artists who shared our concern for the integrity of history and our belief in the profound importance of the Civil War in American history. Only these unspoken beliefs could have taken the time and brought together such scholars as you have collected to assist you in this enterprise.[12]

Thinking back now, I do not believe I misrepresented or exaggerated the true feelings of my colleagues.

2

Ken Burns's The Civil War *as an Interpretation of History*

ROBERT BRENT TOPLIN

*T*HE STORY OF THE CIVIL WAR evidently intrigues the American viewing public considerably, since four particularly influential productions in the history of film and television dealt with issues related to the war. D.W. Griffith's 1915 production *The Birth of a Nation* quickly became a classic. This multi-reel drama about the Civil War and Reconstruction in the South was tremendously popular as well as controversial. Then, David Selznick's 1939 technicolor epic about the Old South, *Gone With the Wind*, turned Margaret Mitchell's popular book into one of Hollywood's most successful and memorable movies. In 1976 David Wolper's *Roots* established a new record for audience size for a television program (the previous record had been established during the television premiere of *Gone With the Wind*). *Roots* carried a story of a slave family through the antebellum period and into the years of the Civil War and emancipation. Then, in 1990, Ken Burns made television history with his eleven-hour documentary on the Civil War. No PBS Television special on history had attracted as much enthusiasm and interest.

These four films did not simply tell interesting stories about the period of the Civil War; they presented interpretations of the American experience. Each used the medium of film to suggest messages about heroes and villains, accomplishments and failures, right and wrong. For example, *The Birth of a Nation* offered a highly biased view of the fall of the Old South and the subsequent exploitation of defeated southerners by supposedly venal Yankee carpetbaggers and their African-American comrades. Griffith's movie portrayed the Ku Klux Klan as savior of the southern whites' way of life. Not surprisingly, African-Americans assailed the movie's interpretation of history. *Gone With the Wind* also presented a favorable picture of the Old South, but its messages about the Yankees and the blacks were not as transparently prejudiced as the portrayals in *The Birth of a Nation*. *Gone With the Wind* offered an idyllic view of conditions on a southern plantation (Tara) and suggested that American society lost an important cultural tradition when the war destroyed a life of gentility. *Roots*, in turn, completely challenged the view of slavery presented in a movie such as *The Birth of a Nation*. It depicted a life of oppression and tragedy for the slaves, and sympathized strongly with the African-Americans yearning for freedom.

While it is not difficult to discern the principal points of view in these dramas, it is somewhat more challenging to identify the perspective in Ken Burns's television series. A fine documentary program such as *The Civil War* does not, on its face, appear to have a point of view. Rather, it leaves the impression of having provided a balanced, objective account of the wartime experience. The series narrator, David McCullough, appears to speak with a voice of professional responsibility and authority, seeming to relate facts about people and events without partisanship. Other figures in the film, such as the southern white historian Shelby Foote, and the Yale and Harvard-trained black historian Barbara Fields, provide additional perspectives. They offer different emphases, but considered together they seem to demonstrate the film's commitment to balance. In short, *The Civil War* has the look of an accurate and fair accounting of the war years. It looks like a visual textbook.

Viewers who are sophisticated in the techniques of filmmaking recognize, however, that documentaries do not really present a non-partisan rendering of history. They understand that no documentary film can be truly value free and objective. A filmmaker such as Ken Burns imposes his personality and philosophy in the production process. He brings to the project a set of assumptions about problems and achievements in modern-day American life and the sources of those conditions as they can be traced through history. In short, he does not approach his material from a neutral position; his personal world-view influences the lessons he draws from history.

This element of bias is manifested in the way a filmmaker selects evidence. Choice is fundamental in the filmmaker's work with sources. For example, Ken Burns encountered thousands of "facts" about the war in the form of pictures, letters, statistics, maps, and other kinds of evidence. He could easily have turned his eleven-hour documentary into a 100-hour or 200-hour film, and still he would have to leave out much interesting material. But Burns made choices. He had to decide which evidence seemed particularly important for the story he wanted to tell. Just by selecting specific examples for presentation on the screen, Burns effectively took a stand in explaining the Civil War to the public. Through the juxtaposition of photographic images that prompted particular emotions, the selection of words for a narration that implied judgments, the inclusion of historians' commentaries at critical points in the analysis, the use of music suggesting particular moods, the employment of sound to create a feeling for a specific situation, he fashioned interpretations of history.

To recognize these biases, viewers should consider the subtle and direct ways that *The Civil War* delivers messages. They should ask, for example: How does the documentary convey an interpretation of history? Do its photographs and narration suggest a romantic view of the war? A critical one? Do the quotations from historical figures imply positive or negative images of the North and South? Who are the heroes in the story, and who are the villains? What are the lessons about the causes of the war and the war's impact on American society? What messages does the film suggest for our own times? Which techniques does the filmmaker use to persuade viewers to share his outlook?

Evaluating Burns's relationship with history is, to a degree, like assessing the way historians of the printed word interpret the past. Both the scholar and the filmmaker select evidence with an eye to materials that they consider relevant to the story they wish to tell, and they shape that evidence in ways that guide their audiences toward particular conclusions. In this respect Burns may be described as a historian as well as a filmmaker (perhaps he should be succinctly identified as a "filmmaker/historian"). To communicate his interpretation Burns employs the modern electronic media rather than just the printed word, but his task is *somewhat* similar to the work of the scholar who reaches audiences through books and articles. There are differences between written history and filmed history, of course (some of them were discussed in the Introduction to this book), but for the moment, it is useful to observe an important similarity.

One of the central issues scholars raise in evaluating written history concerns the ways conditions in the present may influence an author's view of the past, and this consideration can be of value in detecting Ken Burns's point of view in *The Civil War*. Often, individuals are motivated to study a subject from history because of their interest in related issues associated with modern times. Historians see connections, perceive relationships, or assume that they may throw greater light on a contemporary problem by identifying its roots in the past. Historians are product of their times, notes Edward Hazlett Carr; they often see the past in terms of the lessons it offers—its relevance for obtaining a better understanding of the present.[1]

This pattern is evident in the historiography of the Civil War. For instance, authors of important books about the causes of the war have often drawn lessons from the past that seemed relevant to audiences in their own times. Before World War II, historians such as Avery Craven and James G. Randall interpreted the Civil War as an unnecessary fight, a problem of emotions running out of control. The war seemed avoidable, a "repressible conflict."[2] Regrets about American involvement in World War I evidently affected this outlook. Many Americans of the interwar period viewed the "Great War" as a foolish slaughter. They thought the Europeans had gone into battle against each other for questionable reasons, and they viewed

American intervention in the conflict as a mistake. This outlook colored their view of the American Civil War, making observers sympathetic to the conclusion that sectional bloodshed had been unnecessary in 1861. Popular opinion changed after World War II, however. America's fight for freedom against fascist oppression evidently had its impact on the interpretations of history. The "Good War" had involved a struggle against the evils of racism and territorial aggrandizement, and in this context consideration of ethical questions seemed to take on heightened importance. Arthur M. Schlesinger, Jr., drew attention to this issue when he wrote about the moral dimensions of the American Civil War. In Schlesinger's view, slavery posed a problem too severe for easy compromises. The differences between North and South were substantial, and the divisions led the country in the direction of an irrepressible conflict.[3] Furthermore, the American dilemma that Gunnar Myrdal wrote about in the 1940s had begun to influence historical writing.[4] In an age when Americans were moving toward a resolution of contradictions between the American Creed of democracy and equality and the southern reality of segregation and inequality it was not surprising that a historian such as Allan Nevins would argue that the issue of slavery in a democracy and the related problem of "race adjustment" in American society were fundamental elements in the coming of the Civil War.[5]

If the historians who interpret the Civil War through books often write with the present in mind, what can be said of Ken Burns's interpretation in film? Which considerations of Burns's times affected his treatment of history? Which concerns of the late 1980s and the early 1990s (the period of planning and production for *The Civil War*) influenced his storytelling?

Three themes relevant to public opinion in late twentieth-century America seem particularly prominent in *The Civil War*. First, the series is informed by the American experience in the Vietnam War. Burns's documentary communicates a strong emotional sense of the tragedy of war. Secondly, the film reflects American sensibilities in the era following the civil rights revolution. It communicates a strong interest in questions about slavery and racial justice. Finally, the documentary reflects the nationalism of a people who were less divided sectionally in the late twentieth century than in their past. It suggests a message about the shared traditions of northerners and southerners.

Perhaps the most memorable lesson of the entire series is that the war was hell on the people who experienced it. No description of a major battle passes on the screen without some reference to the stench of dead bodies, the horror of amputations, or the primitive state of medical care. The camera lingers on photos of limbs stacked in piles and of three eyeless skulls resting together. Audiences learn about the Union officer who examined the carnage at Petersburg and found "old men with silver locks in the trenches side by side with mere boys of 13 or 14." Burns's documentary does not simply report on the winners and losers of individual battles and move on to the next contest; rather, it reflects on the consequences of combat by presenting abundant photographs of fallen soldiers. The film reports the war's heavy price: the death of one-quarter of the South's men of military age and national casualties amounting to approximately 2 percent of the American population. It shows the faces of the young soldiers and encourages viewers to consider the suffering and the pain felt by their families. One of the most memorable moments in the entire series comes near the end of the first program when audiences hear a recitation of the letter Major Sullivan Ballou of the 2nd Rhode Island wrote home to his wife shortly before he died in the first Battle of Bull Run:

> But, O Sarah! if the dead can come back to this earth and flit unseen around those they loved, I shall always be near you; in the gladdest days and in the darkest nights . . . *always always*, and if there be a soft breeze upon your cheek, it shall be my breath, as the cool air fans your throbbing temple, it shall be my spirit passing by. Sarah do not mourn me dead, think I am gone and wait for thee, for we shall meet again. . . .

That emotion-laden document accents Burns's conclusion that the war should be remembered, most of all, not as a romantic engagement but as a terrible human tragedy.

In this respect, *The Civil War* is a film of the post-Vietnam War era. Burns produced his documentary at a time when many Americans lacked confidence that war-making could effectively serve the nation's interests. Americans did sanction a war against Iraq just a year after *The Civil War*'s broadcast, of course, but many Americans registered strong opposition to that decision, and not many were eager for a protracted fight involving ground troops in the Middle East. The memory of Vietnam cast a long shadow over discussions about combat, reminding Americans of the human suffering associated with combat. Americans recalled the fighting in Vietnam as a frustrating experience that produced much pain and little overall gain. Some considered their country's intervention a tragic mistake and regretted the cost in lives, both American and Asian. Others defended the intervention and wished the U.S. government, the press, and the public had been more supportive of the military effort. Whatever their outlook, they had turned particularly sensitive to the difficulties posed by armed conflict between nations.

In this context, Americans were less likely to accept a glamorous historical portrayal of military conflict than previous generations had. Burns understood the mood. He acknowledged that there was a "dark and antiwar" quality in his film's treatment of fighting in the Civil War. Too often war was presented as a "gallant, bloodless myth," he said. "We've forgotten the obvious fact that we murdered each other."[6]

Burns's message corresponded with the interpretations seen in other films about war produced in the era. The signposts were not uniform, of course, and many Rambo-style movies continued to entertain audiences. These adventure films were a different genre, however; they almost always depicted actions and ideals glamorously. War films about specific historical experiences were a different matter. In the 1940s, 1950s, and 1960s, for instance, many of them conveyed gung-ho stories about heroism and good causes (the John Wayne films were archetypical). But, by the late 1980s and early 1990s, evidence appeared of a more reflective attitude toward war in feature films that dealt with historical situations. *Born on the Fourth of July* (1989), for instance, showed how the experience in Vietnam could wreck a young man's life, and it appropriately revealed a copy of the book *All Quiet on the Western Front* in one of its scenes. Similarly, *Glory* (1989) portrayed combat as a brutal and ugly slaughter even though it celebrated the African-Americans' commitment to fighting for the Union and freedom. Clearly, Burns shared a perspective with producers of the post-Vietnam era who intended to reveal the darker side of war. He and other filmmakers reflected the times when fashioning interpretations, often shaping messages in terms of their reading of trends in American opinion as well as communicating their own feelings about critical issues.

A second major theme in Burns's production concerns the central importance of slavery and racial justice in the sectional conflict. Burns interprets the Civil War as essentially a struggle for freedom and notes that the conflict dealt with the fundamentally important question of the future status of African-Americans. The first program reminds viewers of the harsh conditions of slavery in the antebellum South: shack-style living quarters with dirt floors, dysentery and other maladies, work from sunrise to sundown. Photos give evidence of the ugly treatment of bondsmen: we see slaves in neck braces and irons, and the most memorable image of all from this gallery of horrors shows the terribly scarred back of a slave who evidently had taken many lashes. For the nation, slavery was like having a "wolf by the ears," the film notes, because the leaders worried that they could not easily keep it under control or safely let it go. The cotton gin helped to make this "Peculiar Institution" more valuable, for southern planters needed work hands to tend their crops. King Cotton emerged as the South's major source of riches in the early nineteenth century. Burns's documentary then shifts northward, noting the rise of abolitionist sentiment led by figures such as William Lloyd Garrison, Frederick Douglass, and John Brown. The central issue that divides the nation by 1861 clearly is slavery. At key moments in the documentary Barbara Fields tells viewers that the war was fundamentally about freedom and rights. The United States won its independence from Britain with slavery a part of its heritage, she points out. That condition sowed the seeds for future conflict.

The Civil War does provide information to the contrary, details that could be of interest to those who subscribe to other theories about the war's causes and significance, such as the view of a struggle over states' rights, a conflict between an agrarian and an industrial society, and a clash between two different cultures or civilizations. Indeed, the scholars' battle over causation is not over, and today some historians point to the complexity of antebellum politics in the U.S. and insist that it is too simplistic to claim that "Slavery caused the Civil War." In this debate Burns sides with modern-day interpreters such as James M. McPherson, Richard H. Sewell, David M. Potter, and William J. Cooper, Jr., who identify antislavery and proslavery politics as the most important elements in the sectional split.[7] Burns's title for program number one, "1861: The Cause," makes his thesis clear. For him, slavery is the central reason for the fighting.

In this regard Burns's film reflects the sensitivities of a society that had moved a considerable distance in the second half of the twentieth century to integrate African-Americans into the cultural, economic, and political mainstream. By 1990, African-Americans were still a long way from achieving an impressive degree of economic and social equality, but the gains they realized from the civil rights revolution could not be denied. Legal forms of segregation in the South had come tumbling down in the 1950s and 1960s. Schools and colleges across the nation were more integrated. An African-American served on the Supreme Court and several had been elected to Congress. Blacks were also more prominent in business and industry than in decades before. Additionally, public expressions of racial attitudes had changed significantly. In 1990 it was much less acceptable for white Americans to articulate racial prejudice publicly than it had been forty years before.

These developments affected interpretations of history. Many books about the Civil War published after 1950 gave greater emphasis to slavery as a cause of the war than was the case earlier, and they gave more attention to the problem of prejudice in the period of slavery. The nation's growing commitment to racial justice evidently made an impact on historians' interpretations, stirring a plethora of new studies dealing with the record of unequal treatment of blacks in America. The works of historians such as Kenneth M. Stampp and John Blassingame are but a few examples of this new scholarship.[8] Ken Burns operated in this intellectual environment, and his film reflected the perspective of late twentieth-century America. Like many scholars at the time, he considered the fate of African-Americans a critically important part of the story of the Civil War.

The juxtaposition of anti-war and anti-slavery elements in Burns's documentary creates a minor element of contradiction. Burns concludes that the war was terribly bloody but, because it was about slavery and freedom, the fight was worthwhile. To be sure, Burns wishes a non-violent solution to the issue of slavery had been worked out, but he does not deny that a severe problem existed. His film suggests that slavery constituted a national problem that required a resolution in 1861, not later. The film shows the reformers who challenged slavery in a favorable light while also looking critically at the bloodshed their challenge helped to produce.

Although *The Civil War* gives more credence to the view of an irrepressible sectional conflict than a repressible one, it does not deliberately provoke the sectional passions of its viewers. Burns's film is not designed as a partisan assault on Yankee aggression; nor does the film try to blame southerners exclusively for attachment to slavery and for bringing on the war. *The Civil War* is critical of slavery, but it is not negative in its depiction of southerners. It reflects the new nationalism of the late twentieth century, the perspective of a people trying to move beyond sectional differences.

By 1990, American culture had become more homogenized with respect to North-South differences. Americans appeared to be less sectional in their outlook than they had been through much of their earlier history. In the period after World War II, especially, many southerners moved to northern and western cities in response to job opportunities, and many Yankees (business people, sun worshippers, retirees, and others) relocated to the South. Television, movies, and other means of communication also homogenized Americans, subjecting young and old alike to national rather than distinctly sectional stimuli. By 1990, southerners and northerners were much more familiar with each other through the images of the mass media, and they shared many elements of a common culture by following the same musical idols and enjoying the same television programs. The collapse of racial segregation in the South also helped to remove an important element of regional distinctiveness, although, of course, some vestiges of the old ways remained. As a consequence of this homogenization, northerners and southerners were less contemptuous toward each other than they had been before. Yankees could study the Civil War and relate more empathetically to the hardship the southern people suffered in the years of conflict, and southerners could examine the history with less bitterness about the "Damned Yankees" than their ancestors expressed. The Civil War seemed less a question of "them" against "us." By 1990, it looked more like a sad example of brother against brother. The younger generations were not as much Yankees or Johnny Rebs in their hearts; they thought of themselves first as "Americans."

Some southern letter-writers complained to Ken Burns that *The Civil War* expressed a pro-North bias. Related criticisms surfaced in a variety of letters to newspaper editors and in informal discussions in the South. The assumption of bias rested particularly on two conclusions. The first related to *The Civil War*'s emphasis on slavery as the principal cause of the fighting and racial justice as a centrally important issue in the war. Some white southern critics were unhappy with this perspective. They preferred to see the conflict as a struggle between states and the federal government, as a constitutional dispute, or as a problem involving the supposed aggressiveness of the northern industrialized society against an agrarian South. These interpretations appeared to reduce the importance of slavery and prejudice; they made the story seem less disturbing from a moral point of view. The second assumption about bias related to the amount of time Burns devoted to portraying life in the two sections. A number of white southern critics complained that *The Civil War* devoted an inordinate amount of screen time to scenes of Yankee activity. They said the film failed to give equal time to the Confederacy.

The white southerners who made charges of sectional bias were mistaken. In fact, throughout Burns's documentary the effort to transcend sectionalism and present a relatively balanced picture of the leading figures and their motives is abundantly evident. None of the southern leaders comes off as a "bad guy"—not Jefferson Davis nor Stonewall Jackson nor other major figures in the story. Northern generals such as Ulysses S. Grant and Philip Sheridan also look impressive.

William T. Sherman receives praise for his battlefield tactics, and Joshua Lawrence Chamberlain wins accolades for his service at Gettysburg. Robert E. Lee is treated with great respect. "He is a very great general," Shelby Foote observes. "He took long chances, but he took them because he had to . . . The only way to win for Lee was with long chances, and it made him brilliant." Foote also displays admiration for the Confederates' controversial guerrilla warfare expert, Nathan Bedford Forrest. He calls Forrest one of the authentic geniuses of the war (although he and the narrator balance this praise with critical references to Forrest's virulent prejudice toward African-Americans).

The absence of anti-southern bias is particularly evident in the documentary's treatment of Jefferson Davis. The Confederate president has received a lashing from many historians. Several have compared him unfavorably with Lincoln, noting that Davis seemed haughty and severe, failed to communicate with the masses, interfered too frequently in military planning, antagonized his field commanders, supported personal favorites such as the incompetent Braxton E. Bragg, and failed to deal forcefully with serious problems on the home front. Years ago David M. Potter presented this argument in especially dramatic terms by writing, "In the light of Jefferson Davis' conspicuous lack of an instinct for victory, his lack of a drive and thrust for action and results, his failure to define his office in terms of what needed to be accomplished, it hardly seems unrealistic to suppose that if the Union and the Confederates had exchanged presidents with one another, the Confederacy might have won its independence."[9] As in many other matters of interpretation, *The Civil War* lets Shelby Foote have the last word. Davis was not an "icy-cold man," says Foote, but "an outgoing, friendly man, a great family man who loved his wife and children and had an infinite store of compassion." The assault on Davis's record, says Foote, began during and after the war with the southerners who blamed him rather than the generals for the South's failures. It is "as if a gigantic conspiracy was launched" against Davis, Foote observes.

The only real villain among the leading figures in the film is a northern general, George McClellan. *The Civil War* portrays McClellan as arrogant, uncooperative with the President, and mistaken in his inclination to hold back his armies in the Virginia campaign. Burns's film suggests that McClellan could have helped to bring the war to an early close if he had been willing to commit his men to battle. Far too often, the documentary notes, McClellan exaggerated the enemy's strength and made unrealistic demands for reinforcements. Steven W. Sears, adviser to the series and author of a biography of McClellan, agrees with the overall thrust of the *The Civil War*'s treatment of the general, although he counseled against a heavy-handed McClellan-as-villain portrayal during the planning discussions. Burns concedes that McClellan was an attractive subject for criticism in the medium of television; his film's presentation made McClellan "walk the plank." Thus, it is a Yankee, not a southerner, who serves in the hated role of "bad guy."[10]

Southerners who claimed that Burns favored the Yankees by devoting significantly more time to scenes of the Union's military activities than to scenes of the Confederacy's efforts were wrong on this count, too, for they failed to recognize Burns's extraordinary filmmaking achievement in dealing with unequal source materials. The extant photographs were much more abundant for the Union side than for the Confederate.

After the first year of the Civil War, photographic activity in the South dropped dramatically. Chemicals were in short supply, because the Union blockade kept orders from Europe from reaching southern photographers. Despite these limitations, Burns managed to piece together an informative and moving account of life on both the Confederate war front and home front.

Though individuals who wrote to Burns could easily pick out a few minutes from the eleven hours of programming and argue about a pro-North or pro-South bias, an overview of the entire series reveals that the producer made considerable effort to "sell" his product to a diverse audience of late twentieth-century Americans and internationals. *The Civil War* appears to look back on a distant past; it seems to tell modern viewers that the hate that characterized sectional thinking in America in the 1860s was only remotely visible in the 1990s.

Ken Burns's film series, then, was not simply a balanced, unbiased, and "objective" reporting of the Civil War story. No historical film can likely meet such a rigid definition. Every interpretation of evidence is shaped, to a degree, by the ideas of the storyteller and subtle influences of the times. Burns's documentary reflected his personal interests as well as American society's interests of the late twentieth century—the concern for civil rights, a preoccupation with the human costs of war, and a desire to move beyond traditional North-South animosities. *The Civil War* communicated slanted perspectives.

Recognition of the bias does not necessarily suggest severe criticism of the filmmaker's handling of history. After all, much good scholarship is driven by an author's passionate partisanship and an interest in the modern-day relevance of historical subjects. If the author's judgments are informed and sophisticated, the interpretation can very usefully provoke the reader's thinking. Ken Burns made such a contribution through his television series. His rendering of the Civil War conveyed messages that paralleled important trends in recent scholarship and reflected major trends in popular opinion. With considerable intelligence, Burns demonstrated the relevance of the present for shaping an understanding of the past.

3

How Familiarity Bred Success:
Military Campaigns and Leaders
in Ken Burns's The Civil War

GARY W. GALLAGHER

KEN BURNS'S SERIES ON THE Civil War provoked lively debate about its vision of the great American trauma. Especially in the area of military operations and commanders, discussion highlighted a gulf often separating academic historians and the public. Most viewers responded positively to the series, though they disagreed about its relative treatment of North and South, the degree to which it stressed slavery as a cause of secession, and whether it glorified war by emphasizing the bravery and devotion of common soldiers or conveyed an antiwar subtext through repeated shots of bloated corpses and blasted landscapes. Academic historians centered much of their attention on whether Burns spent inordinate time on military campaigns and thereby obscured larger and more important issues. In the procession of battles and generals, believed many academics, viewers probably missed the broader context within which the armies contended for supremacy. Any consideration of Burns's work raises two questions: Did the series properly balance military and nonmilitary topics? Did Burns develop each appropriately?

Most of the discussion to date has centered on the question of balance. In a cover story on what it termed a "stunning television documentary," *Newsweek* remarked that "Fourteen million Americans, more than the entire population of the Confederacy, gave themselves over to 'The Civil War' last week." Most of those viewers likely would have agreed with the editor of *Civil War Times Illustrated*, a widely read popular publication about the war, who wrote that the series "distills—but does not dilute—some of the most complex issues in our national history into a readily understandable form" and "helps set new standards in using the documentary medium to both interpret history and entertain Americans . . ." Good as it was, added this writer, *The Civil War* neglected the battle of South Mountain, Winfield Scott's strategic contribution to Union victory, and other "minor but pertinent pieces" of the military picture. *Blue & Gray Magazine*, a bimonthly published in Columbus, Ohio, similarly called the documentary "powerful, moving, and educational" but asserted the issue of slavery was "extremely over-treated" while military events such as South Mountain and James Harrison Wilson's destructive raid through Alabama in 1865 were ignored. Overall, nonscholarly magazines devoted to the Civil War typically praised the series but complained about errors of fact or omissions concerning specific battles or campaigns.[1]

Academic historians frequently expressed unhappiness with what they perceived as uncritical popular acceptance of Burns's work. Many of their comments betrayed an impatience toward military topics, which they saw as inherently less interesting and important than social and political dimensions of the war. One typical evaluation pronounced the "commercial success of *The Civil War* to be symptomatic of the problem of historical representation in the media" and worried about "the canonization of narrative strategies embedded in the production of such programs" (the latter statement speaks volumes about why so few lay readers find academic history to their taste). Agreeing with others who voiced unhappiness with Burns's "conception of the Civil War as a history of war," this scholar quoted with thinly veiled sarcasm the filmmaker's statement that "'only' 40 percent of the eleven hours depicted battles." "*The Civil War* is luxuriant on military detail and very thin on political context," complained another academic reviewer. "Each major battle is separately portrayed, the character of its generals dissected, and its battlefields, now quiet and reflective, filmed in long, beautiful shots; this is the visual version of the approach taken by generations of Civil War buffs, for whom re-enacting battles is a beloved hobby. Missing are the truly decisive *political* battles, which determined what the armies of the North and South brought to each of their physical confrontations."[2]

Much of the scholarly criticism reflected changes in the historical profession that have brought to the forefront people and issues previously slighted or ignored. The desire to make American history more inclusive and to reveal its ambiguities and tensions certainly is laudable, but I believe it important to remember that the subject of Burns's documentary was a mammoth *war* that unfolded chronologically. Would avoiding chronological narrative and muting the role of armies make the experience of 1861–65 more intelligible to non-specialists?

In their haste to deny the centrality of military events, many of Burns's critics overlook that what occurred on battlefields profoundly influenced virtually every aspect of life behind the lines. Military results often shaped the "truly decisive *political* battles." Neither the home front nor the battlefield can be understood without attention to myriad reciprocal influences that determined actions and decisions in both spheres.

Nor does it help to label readers (or viewers) interested in military campaigns and leaders as "buffs" eager to dress up and restage battles. The vast majority of "buffs" neither has donned a uniform nor attended a Civil War re-enactment. Their interests usually extend well beyond questions of where regiments and brigades fought on individual battlefields. Content to speak to one another in language that excludes almost anyone outside the university community, many academic historians ignore a literate lay audience that consistently has manifested interest in the Civil War. A sense of "we know best" permeates much of their commentary about Burns. Put off by the public's fondness for generals and battles and narrative integrity, these academics insist that lay readers and viewers should be given "real history" as defined by scholars.

In fact, any documentary about the Civil War that failed to place military events at least close to center stage would itself be open to charges of distortion. Moreover, I suspect the notion that any documentary on a cataclysmic conflict should play down the importance of military events would amuse most non-academics. Millions of people North and South eagerly followed the progress of Union and Confederate armies on a daily basis, according more attention to strategic maneuvers and battles than to any of the non-military topics favored by modern scholars. Perceptions about the military situation influenced how people voted, whether they bought government bonds, and many of their other activities. One university professor may have been too harsh when he ascribed "nitpicking" academic criticisms of Burns to jealousy over the commercial success of *The Civil War*; however, he was correct in stating that "Burns has made history live, giving it a human face and vivid texture rarely achieved in Academe." Indeed, Burns's greatest achievement lay in his ability to fire the imaginations of millions of Americans, sending them in large numbers to libraries and bookstores in search of more information.[3]

Many academic scholars revealed their lack of interest in soldiers and battles by questioning how much time Burns spent on the battlefield but never asking how well he covered military events. I have tipped my hand about the first question. I think Burns strikes a reasonable balance between military and non-military coverage. The remainder of my essay will address the soundness of his discussion of military aspects of the war. Does *The Civil War* incorporate recent scholarship? Is the geographical coverage balanced? Are the major actors on each side given appropriate attention? Does Burns evaluate available sources judiciously? And does he strive to explain the connections between the home front and the battlefield? Regrettably, my answers to these questions suggest that the Burns approach is an utterly conventional one that leaves the viewer with a skewed sense of the war's military dimension.[4]

Although Burns consulted a number of prominent historians, many parts of *The Civil War* betray, curiously, an ignorance of modern scholarship. The first episode sets the military stage with a flawed examination of resources at the opening of the conflict. Stressing the North's industrial capacity and vastly larger pool of manpower, Burns concludes that "the odds against a southern victory were long." True as far as it goes, this approach overlooks important Confederate advantages that evened the initial balance sheet. The Confederacy had only to defend itself and could win if the North did nothing; moreover, its armies could stand on the defensive while Union forces faced the task of conquering and occupying the South. The immense size of the Confederacy (at 750,000 square miles double the size of the American colonies during the Revolutionary War) and its 3500-mile coastline posed daunting obstacles to northern arms. In works such as James M. McPherson's *Ordeal by Fire* and *Battle Cry of Freedom* and Herman Hattaway and Archer Jones's *How the North Won*, Burns had readily available analyses of each side's strengths and weaknesses. Inexplicably, he chose to overlook their insights.[5]

Burns's appraisal of resources drapes a mantle of hopelessness over the Confederate resistance, imparting an especially tragic quality to the costly battles that follow. Here *The Civil War* echoes Lost Cause writers such as Jubal A. Early, who often attributed Confederate defeat to the enemy's material strength. Gallant struggle against impossible odds elevated Confederate soldiers, as Early suggested in an 1872 address on R. E. Lee: "General Lee had not been conquered in battle . . . [H]e surrendered . . . the mere ghost of the Army of Northern Virginia, which had been gradually worn down by the combined agencies of numbers, steam-power, railroads, mechanism, and all the resources of physical science." This interpretive tradition extends back to Lee himself, who had assured his soldiers at Appomattox on April 9, 1865, that the enemy's "overwhelming numbers and resources" had compelled him to surrender.[6]

Other passages reinforce the initial image of badly outnumbered Confederates. In Episode III, for example, Burns describes Lee's army on June 26, 1862, as a "tiny force" facing a juggernaut in George B. McClellan's Army of the Potomac. The ensuing Seven Days battles assume the character of an underdog southern force vanquishing a much larger but inept opponent—a conception at odds with the facts. When Lee took charge of Confederate troops outside Richmond in early June 1862 he summoned reinforcements from many quarters. By the end of the month, he commanded approximately 90,000 soldiers in the largest army ever fielded by the Confederacy. Although McClellan's Federals outnumbered the Confederates by 10,000 to 15,000 men, Lee came nearer to parity with his opponent than in any subsequent operation. Far from a mismatch, the Seven Days witnessed two roughly equal antagonists square off on ground that should have favored the Confederates.[7]

The series similarly misrepresents the impact of technology on late-antebellum American military officers. Following his segment in Episode II on the slaughter at Shiloh, which details how the battle's horrific casualties shocked civilians on both sides, Burns takes up the topic of technological advances. Viewers learn that the "most important innovation of the whole war was the rifled musket, along with a French refinement, Captain Claude Minié's new bullet, an inch-long lead slug that expanded into the barrel's rifled grooves and spun as it left the muzzle" and "was accurate at 250 yards, five times as far as any other one-man weapon." "The age of the bayonet charge had ended," announces the narrator, "though most officers did not yet know it when the war began and some had not learned it when the war was over."

This narration and the juxtaposition of graves at Shiloh with the new weaponry mislead viewers by suggesting that Civil War officers first contemplated rifle-muskets and minié balls during the war. The United States Army had converted from smoothbores to rifle-muskets in the mid-1850s, necessitating revision of the tactical manuals to cope with the weapon's increased distance and accuracy. "The introduction of the rifle had produced changes in tactical thinking," noted Grady McWhiney and Perry D. Jamieson in an excellent summary of late-antebellum developments, "but the changes were not extensive enough to compensate for the firepower of the new weapon." Official army doctrine thus recognized a new tactical era well before the cannons fired at Fort Sumter in April 1861. Although the war saw many costly infantry assaults at Shiloh and elsewhere, their outcome cannot be explained as mistakes by officers innocent of the improved weaponry.[8]

The most obvious shortcoming of Burns's military coverage concerns geographical imbalance. His war is pre-eminently a struggle between the famous armies that operated in Virginia and the rest of the Eastern Theater. For the purpose of this essay, it is crucial to state here that Burns neither justifies his emphasis on the East nor acknowledges the views of historians who complain of a Virginia bias. Apparently unconcerned with how people at the time perceived the relative importance of campaigns in the East and West (and perhaps influenced by the richer store of photographs of Eastern armies and battlefields), he seems to take as a given the greater importance of military operations in Virginia, Maryland, and Pennsylvania. In doing so he again follows a Lost Cause tradition exemplified artistically by Charles Hoffbauer's famous murals depicting the "Seasons of the Confederacy." Gracing one gallery of the Virginia Historical Society in Richmond, the murals equate Virginia with the Confederacy: "Spring" depicts Stonewall

Jackson's infantry on the march in the Shenandoah Valley; "Summer" a tableau of Lee and his generals on a Virginia hillside; "Autumn" a ragged line of troopers following "Jeb" Stuart amid blazing fall colors; and "Winter" a Confederate artillery battery going into action at snowy Fredericksburg.

I happen to believe that during the war events in the East did overshadow those beyond the Appalachians. European political leaders, many politicians in Washington, and civilians in the Union and the Confederacy most often looked to Virginia to gauge the war's progress. The presence of the opposing capitals and each side's largest army, as well as the increasingly dominant figure of R. E. Lee, helps to explain this phenomenon. Psychologically and politically, what happened in the Eastern Theater heavily influenced both sides. Lee and the Army of Northern Virginia came to embody the Confederacy in the minds of many southern whites. So long as they remained in the field, hopes for Confederate independence remained alive. Similarly, victories in the West could not counter the North's frustration with repeated defeats at Lee's hands. The northern public insisted in March 1864 that Ulysses S. Grant, recently made general-in-chief of the Union armies, take the field in Virginia, hoping their best general would inflict defeat on the rebel chieftain.[9]

I hasten to add that many scholars dispute the primacy of the Eastern Theater. Thomas L. Connelly, Archer Jones, Richard M. McMurry, and others have complained of an undue preoccupation with the East in too much military literature on the war, arguing that Union achievements in the West largely decided the contest. Beginning with the capture of Confederate Fort Henry and Fort Donelson in early 1862 and progressing through victories at Shiloh, Vicksburg, and Chattanooga to Sherman's success in Georgia and the Carolinas in 1864–65, northern armies gutted the logistical heartland of the Confederacy, crippled civilian morale, and rendered further struggle impossible. Anyone searching for the key to northern victory, insist these authors, must look outside Virginia.[10]

How pronounced is the Eastern thrust of *The Civil War*? The best evidence concerns Gettysburg and Vicksburg, for which Burns followed popular impressions rather than the scholarly literature. Historians often describe the Union triumphs at Gettysburg and Vicksburg as twin calamities for the Confederacy. The one repulsed Lee's second raid across the Potomac River and inflicted stupendous losses on the Army of Northern Virginia, the other gave the North control of the Mississippi River and removed an entire Confederate army from the field. "We have certain information that Vicksburg surrendered to General Grant on the 4th of July," a joyful Abraham Lincoln wrote on July 7, 1863: "Now, if General Meade can complete his work, so gloriously prosecuted thus far [at Gettysburg], by the literal or substantial destruction of Lee's army, the rebellion will be over." James M. McPherson echoed many other historians in observing that "the losses at Gettysburg and Vicksburg shook the Confederacy to its foundations." A concomitant Federal success in the West, William S. Rosecrans's virtually bloodless maneuvering of Braxton Bragg and the Army of Tennessee out of Middle Tennessee during the Tullahoma campaign of June–July 1863, added to laurels won by U. S. Grant at Vicksburg.[11]

Despite these major Union victories along the Mississippi River and in the Confederate heartland, Burns elected to reinforce the common misconception that Gettysburg dominated that remarkable season of combat. He lavishes nearly 45 minutes on the campaign in Pennsylvania versus fewer than eleven on the marching and fighting between December 1862 and July 1863 that settled Vicksburg's fate. Rosecrans's Tullahoma campaign, which helped set the stage for the Union advance from Chattanooga to Atlanta in 1864, garners not a single mention.

Treatment of other operations reflects a similar bias. Strategic offensives in late summer and fall 1862 marked the only time Confederates armies penetrated Union territory in the Eastern and Western theaters almost simultaneously. Lee's march into Maryland and the battle of Antietam (the Eastern element of these offensives) receive 25 minutes, movements into Kentucky by Confederate forces under Braxton Bragg and Edmund Kirby Smith (the Western component) only fleeting attention. Similarly, Episode IV allocates a 12-minute section to Lee's battle at Fredericksburg, Virginia, in December 1862, while the clash at Murfreesboro, Tennessee, a bloodier Western counterpart fought on December 31, 1862, and January 2, 1863, winks past viewers in less than a minute. When Ulysses S. Grant planned his five-pronged advance against the Confederacy in the spring of 1864, he considered William Tecumseh Sherman's strike against Atlanta the first priority and his own campaign against Lee a secondary element designed to tie down and bleed Confederate forces in Virginia. Burns inexplicably reverses this ranking, stating that "Grant entrusted his friend with the second most important part of his grand strategy—to seize Atlanta and smash the combined Confederate armies of Tennessee and Mississippi under Joseph E. Johnston."

The Trans-Mississippi Theater fares worst of all the geographical areas. Burns disregards Pea Ridge and Wilson's Creek (except for mentioning casualties at the latter), battles that helped decide the fate of Missouri, a slaveholding state Lincoln believed must be held if the Union were to be preserved. Similarly, viewers learn nothing about Henry Hopkins Sibley's Confederate invasion of New Mexico in 1862, Nathaniel P. Banks's Federal advance up the Red River in the spring of 1864, Confederate general Sterling Price's raid into Missouri later that year, and numerous other noteworthy military events west of the Mississippi. Episode VII does furnish a glimpse of Missouri's brutal guerrilla war in a snippet about the vicious Confederate irregular "Bloody Bill" Anderson. Shelby Foote apparently failed to influence Burns regarding the Trans-Mississippi. The documentary's neglect of that sprawling region contrasts sharply with Foote's own narrative history of the Civil War, which apportions it a generous number of pages.[12]

Even when engaged with the Eastern Theater, Burns often follows hoary interpretive conventions that obscure almost as much as they reveal. He reduces the battle of Fredericksburg to the infamous slaughter of Union attackers below the Sunken Road on Marye's Heights, offering no substantive attention to action on the southern end of the field where Union troops achieved some success against "Stonewall" Jackson's defenders. Gettysburg supplies a number of comparable examples. Traditionally given far less attention than either of the other two days, the first day's fighting appears in Episode V as "a skirmish" compared with what was to come. Burns thus brushes aside a compelling meeting engagement that escalated into savage combat claiming thousands of Union and Confederate casualties. He offers equally predictable emphases for the rest of the battle. The Federal defense of Little Round Top dominates coverage of the second day, with action at the

Peach Orchard, Wheatfield, and Devil's Den playing decidedly secondary roles and the contest for Culp's Hill altogether absent. The climactic Confederate assault on the third day is "Pickett's Charge," leaving uninformed viewers with the impression that George E. Pickett and his division of Virginians made up all (rather than considerably less than half) of the assaulting column and that Pickett rather than James Longstreet oversaw the Confederate effort.

Perhaps Burns's deep admiration for Michael Shaara's novel *The Killer Angels* contributed to this unbalanced treatment of Gettysburg. Of the characters Shaara featured on July 1, only John Buford, whose Federal cavalry gave way to supporting infantry before the battle escalated, actively participated in the fighting. Shaara built his account of the second day's fighting around Joshua Lawrence Chamberlain and the 20th Maine on Little Round Top and used Lewis A. Armisted and his brigade in Pickett's division to take readers through the final Confederate assault on July 3.[13]

Several sections on the war in the East demonstrate Burns's capacity to rise above trite conceptions—which renders the weaker passages all the more frustrating. With Stonewall Jackson's 1862 Shenandoah Valley campaign, for example, Burns avoids the ubiquitous stereotype of 17,000 rugged Confederate "foot cavalrymen" defeating more than 60,000 Federals. No extravagant claims accompany the treatment of how Jackson bested several inept Union generals and tied down some 40,000 enemy troops while strategists in Richmond worked to stop George B. McClellan's advance up the Peninsula.

Robert E. Lee, Ulysses S. Grant, and William Tecumseh Sherman rightly dominate Burns's cast of generals. Collectively, the three wielded far greater influence on military affairs than any of their peers. Could the Confederacy have mounted a four-year resistance without Lee's ability to build and sustain morale through battlefield victories? Was ultimate Union success possible without the strategic and operational contributions of Grant and Sherman? A positive answer to either question strains credulity.

Having selected the three key military figures, however, Burns fails to follow through with satisfying portraits. The film serves up a very traditional profile of Lee replete with venerable inaccuracies. Episode I tells viewers that he opposed slavery—a correct statement only if one applies the most expansive definition of "antislavery." Episode V repeats a common misconception that after the second day's fighting at Gettysburg, Lee believed an all-out attack on the Federal center would carry the field; he actually planned strikes against both Federal flanks and settled for the option of a frontal attack only with great reluctance on the morning of July 3. The biographical sketch in Episode VI alludes to Lee's habitually referring to Federals as "those people" rather than the enemy. Even a cursory canvass of Lee's own writings, which bristle with references to Federals as "the enemy," would have spared Burns this last error.[14]

Nowhere does the series take up questions about Lee's generalship that have inspired vigorous debate over many decades. Did his strategic grasp serve the Confederacy well, or was he blinded by a determination to protect his native Virginia? Did the benefits of his legendary victories outweigh their terrible price in casualties? How did Confederate civilians respond to his battles and campaigns? Did he and his army divert attention from more important events in the West? What was his ultimate impact on the fortunes of the Confederacy? Shelby Foote turns a nice phrase in observing that "Gettysburg was the price the South paid for having Robert E. Lee," but such statements are a poor substitute for analysis. In the end, viewers see an aristocratic, bountifully gifted officer who wins most of his battles and confronts defeat with dignity. Both Lee and Burns's audience deserved a more sophisticated treatment.[15]

The relationship between U. S. Grant and William Tecumseh Sherman forms an appealing leitmotif in the documentary. Burns understands the importance of this most productive professional collaboration of the war but fails to stress Grant's dominant role in the partnership. During a period of early independent command, Sherman had been beset by doubts and fears of the enemy. Grant's steadiness and unshakable commitment to victory freed his mercurial lieutenant to blossom as a successful field commander. Cognizant that he functioned as the subordinate member of this team, Sherman perceptively summarized the strengths that he and his fellow Ohioan brought to command: "I am a damned sight smarter man than Grant; I know a great deal more about war, military history, strategy, and grand tactics than he does; I know more about organization, supply, and administration and about everything else than he does; but I'll tell you where he beats me and where he beats the world. He don't care a damn for what the enemy does out of his sight, but it scares me like hell!" In March 1864, as Grant prepared to assume responsibility for all Union land forces, Sherman revealed how important his friend's reassuring presence had been during previous campaigns. "I knew wherever I was that you thought of me," he wrote Grant, "and if I got in a tight place you would come—if alive."[16]

Through Shelby Foote, Burns characterizes Sherman as perhaps the first "modern" general because he realized war on civilians would mark future conflicts. In fact, well before Sherman began his "March to the Sea" in November 1864, Grant had formulated a strategy of exhaustion that targeted the logistical underpinnings of the Confederacy. Philip H. Sheridan cheerfully carried out Grant's orders to apply this strategic concept to the Shenandoah Valley in October 1864. "Do all the damage to railroads and crops you can," read Grant's instructions. "Carry off stock of all descriptions, and negroes, so as to prevent further planting. If the war is to last another year, we want the Shenandoah Valley to remain a barren waste." Sheridan's soldiers subsequently destroyed huge quantities of civilian property in what embittered Confederates called "The Burning."[17]

The Union's military effort in the West belongs to Grant and Sherman in *The Civil War*, leaving other prominent Federal officers unfairly in the shadows. John Charles Frémont, Don Carlos Buell, and William S. Rosecrans all held important Western commands but play only the smallest of bit parts in the documentary. The most blatant omission concerns Henry W. Halleck, whom Burns casts briefly as a jealous administrator hoping to push Grant aside after Shiloh. Halleck's strategic and organizational skills, as well as his ability to select able subordinates, brought Union victories that cleared rebels from Missouri, made deep inroads into Arkansas, and captured immensely rich logistical areas in western and middle Tennessee. At the time, Grant called Halleck "one of the greatest men of the age" and Sherman pronounced him the "directing genius" behind Union successes in the West during the winter and spring of 1862. Halleck's achievements earned him promotion to general-in-chief of the Union armies in July 1862; however, frustration and failure in that position tarnished his earlier accomplishments and colored most subsequent estimates of his abilities. Apparently distracted by Halleck's career in Washington, Burns overlooked his splendid earlier service.[18]

On the Confederate side, viewers might infer that cavalryman Nathan Bedford Forrest ranked as the most important officer in the West. Shelby Foote relates a number of colorful anecdotes about the roughhewn general and, incredibly, places him alongside Abraham Lincoln as one of the war's "two authentic geniuses." Although Forrest never commanded more than a few thousand men, his appearances in the series outnumber those of Braxton Bragg, Albert Sidney Johnston, Joseph E. Johnston, P. G. T. Beauregard, and others who led southern armies during major campaigns. This treatment grossly inflates Forrest's prominence. His wartime contemporaries in the Confederacy typically saw Forrest as a peer of John Hunt Morgan and Earl Van Dorn, other successful raiders whose exploits vexed the Federals, but scarcely conceived of him as a general whose impact rivaled that of senior officers.[19] Northerners loathed Forrest because of the slaughter of black and white troops who surrendered to his men at Fort Pillow in April 1864 (to his credit, Burns does not play down this episode in Forrest's career) and probably wished him dead—few, however, considered him a threat to the Republic equivalent to the Army of Tennessee under Braxton Bragg or Joseph E. Johnston.

Brevity and predictability characterize Burns's portrayal of other generals, encouraging viewers, perhaps inadvertently, to adopt simplistic notions about officers whose careers invite a more layered understanding. John Pope and Joseph E.

Johnston illustrate this phenomenon. Burns's Pope is the posturing braggart familiar even to casual students of the war. Pope may have blustered (though he did not habitually locate his "headquarters in the saddle," as the film claims), but he was more than a buffoon. His actions in northern Virginia during August 1862 reflected a shift in Union policy toward a harsher style of war embracing private property and civilians as well as Confederate armies. Johnston comes across as an avuncular figure who looked after his soldiers and skillfully husbanded meager southern resources. Although Johnston may have been "very nearly worshiped by his men" during his withdrawal from north Georgia to Atlanta in May and June 1864, many civilians, politicians, and others in the Confederacy deplored his constant retreating and insisted on a more active opposition to Sherman. John Bell Hood understood why Jefferson Davis substituted him for Johnston in mid-July and immediately mounted an offensive. In these and many other cases, the addition of political and social context to a military discussion—which is very different, I should emphasize, from a reduction of the amount of military coverage—would have strengthened Burns's work.[20]

Throughout the series Burns missed opportunities to show that generals cannot operate in a vacuum during a war between democratic societies. The allocation of resources, selection of targets, appointment of officers, definition of operational goals, and timing of campaigns often represented a compromise between military and political imperatives. Lincoln waited until after the elections in November 1862 to remove the popular George B. McClellan (a staunch Democrat); kept political generals such as Nathaniel P. Banks and Benjamin F. Butler in command despite their well-documented ineptitude; postponed his preliminary proclamation of emancipation until he had a victory in the Eastern Theater; and otherwise adjusted his military goals to suit political realities. Similarly, Jefferson Davis deployed precious men and material to defend peripheral areas because civilians in those regions demanded protection.

Generals bowed to public opinion on numerous occasions, as when Grant took the field against Lee in April 1864 and Lee removed the unpopular Jubal A. Early from command in the Shenandoah Valley in March 1865. Political constraints also affected officers in the field. Generals John C. Frémont and David Hunter, while Federal commanders in Missouri in 1861 and along the south Atlantic coast in 1862 respectively, issued sweeping orders emancipating slaves only to have Lincoln insist that he alone possessed the authority for such actions. Sometimes these connections stand out in *The Civil War*—the relation between Antietam and the Emancipation Proclamation is one example—but more often than not generals and their armies appear to operate in an environment devoid of nonmilitary pressures.

The correlation between events on the battlefield and morale behind the lines also remains underdeveloped. Lee's stunning triumphs in 1862–63 convinced many white southerners (as well as a number of soldiers in the Army of the Potomac) that he could not be beaten. For the rest of the war, an expectation of success from the Army of Northern Virginia helped maintain Confederate morale as southern arms suffered setbacks almost everywhere else. The Army of the Potomac's string of losses more than once spread turmoil through northern society. Defeats at the Seven Days and Second Bull Run triggered a diplomatic crisis, another pair of setbacks at Fredericksburg and Chancellorsville fueled support for the antiwar Copperheads, and Grant's inability to deliver a knockout blow to Lee's army during May and June 1864 helped drive northern morale to its lowest point of the conflict. Specific development of these connections between the battlefield and the home front would have formed a useful theme in Burns's documentary, while also deflecting complaints that he gave too much attention to the military.

The common denominator for most of my criticisms lies in Burns's failure to sift carefully through the best literature on the war. Much of his material comes from highly quotable but problematical postwar memoirs and reminiscences such as Sam Watkins's "*Co. Aytch*" and John B. Gordon's *Reminiscences of the Civil War*. Storehouses of comfortable old stories that undoubtedly move audiences when told well, these books cluster toward the bottom on any scale of reliability. Some manipulate the truth to even old scores or place their author in the best light; others simplify and sanitize issues and leaders—especially if, like Gordon's book, they appeared during the era of sectional reconciliation. A systematic use of modern scholarship would have provided a check on these older accounts and enabled Burns to avoid many errors and distortions. I am not arguing that *The Civil War* should have adopted a scholarly format. That would have driven viewers off in droves as surely as dry historiographical lectures send students reeling from college classrooms. But with the latitude afforded by an eleven-hour format, Burns could have injected more complexity into his military narrative and his sketches of leading soldiers while still including an ample number of fetching anecdotes.

I will not dwell on the numerous small errors that litter the narrative. William Tecumseh Sherman was not orphaned as a young boy; John Singleton Mosby was not a general; the British observer with Lee's army at Gettysburg was A.J.L. (not A.S.) Fremantle; an image of Federal wagons parked on the Peninsula in 1862 does not belong in the sequence on Gettysburg, and so on. The cumulative effect of these lapses somewhat weakens the informed viewer's confidence and prompts the wish that a scholar had given the final script a careful proofreading, but I do not believe such errors materially compromise the documentary.

My critique will strike many viewers of *The Civil War* as unduly harsh. It may seem to be another piece of academic carping about a popular success. Such is not the case. I applaud Burns for taking on such a monumental and potentially controversial subject when he must have anticipated intense scrutiny from both academics and the public. He brought to the project a record of superb documentary filmmaking and acquired the funding to approach the Civil War on an expansive scale. He sought the advice of historians, searched for the right nineteenth-century and modern images, and must have read widely in the literature. He settled on a good balance between military and non-military coverage. With so many crucial elements in place, the likelihood of success was great.

My disappointment stems from a sense of missed opportunity. Burns could have used his undeniable narrative gifts to present the broad context as well as the drama and pathos of military campaigns. Instead, he maneuvered comfortably along well-trod paths, employing durable anecdotes, serving up leaders in familiar interpretive garb, and never challenging his viewers with choices or enabling them to see how campaigns and battles merged with civilian affairs to create a magnificent historical tapestry.

4

"Noble Women as Well"

CATHERINE CLINTON

*W*HEN KEN BURNS'S PHENOMENAL series appeared on PBS in the fall of 1990, millions of viewers sat with eyes glued to their television sets each and every night. By fax, phone, and at water coolers, people hotly debated Burns's project. In many faculty lounges, Burns's "popularization" was lauded, although too many historians, especially those who consistently take pride in the obscurity of their subjects and the impenetrability of their prose, were distinctly disgruntled.

I noticed the day after the first episode, my students at Harvard in Afro-American Studies were indifferent; I had suggested—but not required—they watch. Most confessed they had not bothered to tune in; some started watching, but after a while, switched it off. Several rationalized they *knew* black issues would be slighted by any program gushed over by the media in the lavish way that Burns's project had been. Their skepticism combined the best sort of insight and ignorance which undergraduates consistently display: as one student complained, he didn't expect to learn anything "from a guy who looked like Opie."

I argued that we should not make such superficial judgments. Nor even condemn Burns solely on the basis of his opening episode, designed to engage a first-night audience with stark images and powerful words, beguiling us with music and emotion. Who could not be mesmerized by David McCullough's dulcet tones and the reading of a poignant excerpt from Sullivan Ballou's last letter to his wife, accompanied by mournful violins? Once hooked, I was sure Burns's "line and sinker" would be more substantial. He'd reel us in with the diversity of his on-camera experts: from the drawling charm of Shelby Foote to the political co-rectitude of Barbara Fields. In future episodes, Burns would not simply mount the ramparts and let cannons roar, punching the macho hot buttons that have kept Civil War literature a popular staple for the past century. I knew he would responsibly intercut testosterone-laced legends with emerging views of blacks, women, the home front—wouldn't he? *Wouldn't he?*

It was with a heavy heart that I watched the hours roll by and an even sadder moment when the closing minutes once and for all sealed the case. Those images of a re-enactment of Pickett's Charge in 1913 sentimentalized the theme of reconciliation, providing a folksy and comfortable closure for white Americans—and a racialized distortion of the war's meaning. Burns sold emancipation down the river. Ken Burns wanted us to feel good about the Civil War—but which "us" was he thinking of? Yes, Civil War veterans did gather together and celebrate reconciliation. But they stood in metaphorical formation, during what one scholar has called "the nadir of American race relations."

If Ken Burns asks for our attention for eleven hours, then scholars rightly claim foul when his selectivity seems so imbalanced or the lack of context produces myopic distortion. These legitimate arguments can be productively debated.[1] (Burns's slights concerning race have been dealt with at length by others.[2]) Sins of omission, however, are not equal to propaganda.

When I expressed my admiration for Burns's ability to touch his audience at a panel on film and history, and confessed that at times I was moved to tears by the poignancy of some of *The Civil War*'s images, a member of the audience berated me with a rejoinder that in Germany today young neo-Nazis weep over the films of Leni Riefenstahl. Again and again, I am willing to join in critical discussion of this project, but the shrillness of Burns's critics steers me away from the camp of his detractors and into the realm of fan.

At the same time, Burns's repeated references to working on this project for five years grated. I'm sure it took that long, but he could have spent a little more time proofreading the script, where howling errors cropped up regularly: over the number of teen-aged enlistees, over the average life span of blacks—and other details, minor but *telling* mistakes. Such gaffes horrified historians, myself included.[3]

Burns cannot be blamed for the misquotes the press frequently commit, but his on-camera rapture and being cast as Homer for America's own *Iliad* invited sharp response.[4] Burns's coronation gave many struggling and established academics palpitations. Historians feared that Burns's project would become the "last word," and government and corporate funding on the topic would dry up. His vision of the Civil War would "dominate." This was not an irrational fear, but more than five years later such concerns have proven unwarranted. *Au contraire*, Burns created a mini-boom from which historians have benefited since his program aired. Many of us, whether we like it or not, owe Ken Burns a debt of gratitude.

This documentary *Wunderkind* has rejuvenated serious interest in history—from networks, corporations, and, perhaps, even the viewing public. Burns's historical influence has brought people back to reading (or at least buying!) more books, created a vogue in Civil War scholarship (especially for the new media darling, Shelby Foote), and launched numerous projects at libraries and state humanities commissions across the country. Our students, our readership, and the entire enterprise of bringing history to the people have profited. This very volume symbolizes his impact. We must salute him, even as some may seek to bury him.

Now that I've coated Burns in honey (compared with many colleagues' vinegar dip), I want him tied to the stake for a while. For all of my gratitude and sincere admiration, I think Burns deserves a slow painful punishment for his "boys will be boys" coyness and his lapses concerning women.[5]

My concerns must be distinguished from most others in this volume which are rightfully "academic criticism." Mine are not. Far from it. In fact, Burns was just one of the Good Ole Boys who from the Little Rascals clubhouse to the ivy-covered academic halls practice ancient ritual: NO WOMEN ALLOWED.[6] Such critiques are frequently dismissed as "feminist" by both scholars and media—translating into "let her talk but don't bother to listen." Burns has demonstrated that when it comes to women, he not only doesn't get it, he doesn't seem to care.

The Civil War's wholesale neglect of women—black and white, northern and southern, nurses and spies, disguised in uniform or on the home front—is not an oversight. Burns had the material to integrate women fully into his story and chose not to. Considering his own perspective and criteria, this was a wasted opportunity, which might be summarized: "Mrs. Sullivan Ballou, where are you?"[7]

It was "poignantly" pointed out in several print media that Sarah Ballou lost her husband at Bull Run and "never remarried." The sentiments mistakenly attached to this statement never cease to amuse me: how likely was it she could remarry when a generation of men were wiped out? She struggled along with hundreds of thousands of war widows, trying to raise her children—years later probably able to claim a pension to help her survive the terrible ordeal. Women of her generation were robbed of their youth, their security, their hopes, their dreams dashed by a husband's vainglorious demise. More likely, women had Scarlett O'Hara's luck with her first husband— died of dysentery before ever seeing battle. And Sullivan Ballou's wife was fortunate because, unlike the beleaguered Scarlett, her husband's side won. Confederate widows suffered with no government relief forthcoming.

As I studiously viewed and reviewed eleven hours of Burns's *Civil War,* women were all but invisible, all but silent in the finished film—as my notes attest:

- EPISODE I: "The Cause"—included references or quotes for Harriet Tubman, Harriet Beecher Stowe, Mary Chesnut, and Varina Davis.

- EPISODE II: "A Very Bloody Affair"—zip
- EPISODE III: "Forever Free"—Susie King Taylor, a black woman's voice. Quote from Clara Barton which is a "local color" battlefield quote. Very florid material on blacks, mainly men.
- EPISODE IV: "Simply Murder"—Bread Riot, mention of women. "Lorena" is a popular song on both sides—only women are in songs?
- EPISODE V: "The Universe of Battle"—black woman on camera, Daisy Turner, daughter of black soldier—battle related. Chapter Six: "SHE RANKS ME" nurses, back on the farm, Sanitary Commission—fluffy
- EPISODE VI: "Valley of Death"—zip
- EPISODE VII: "Most Hallowed Ground"—usual prostitute ref.: women as "horizontal refreshments."
- EPISODE VIII: "War Is All Hell"—unidentified women's voices on Sherman's March segment. No reference to women's letters.
- EPISODE IX: "The Better Angels of Our Nature"—woman's voice on surrender—unidentified. "Whatever happened" covers Mary Todd Lincoln, Clara Barton, Julia Ward Howe(???), and Mary Chesnut.

I used to attribute the absence of women in such books and projects to laziness and ignorance. Burns provides too little, too late when he admits—in Episode V, Chapter Six—that females mobilized in ways that were crucial to winning the war. Unfortunately the selective eye of the creator and editors excluded material featuring women, in an overwhelming if not systematic fashion, in *The Civil War*.

As Nina Silber and I argued in *Divided Houses*, Civil War history and women's history remain two fields which have too long conspired to remain mutually exclusive domains. In a re-verse "devil's lane" (the disputed tract of land between two properties), the study of women during the Civil War has become the *neglected* patch between—which both fail to claim. Scholars on both sides have been content to cast aspersions, wishing ill to those across the fence. But as we move toward a more mature process of re-evaluation and appreciation, this dynamic and dramatic historical legacy has much to offer: a profusion of rich material unfolds. Dozens of dissertations and monographs are in the works and vibrant volumes of letters, diaries, and journals pour into print with each passing year.

Burns should be consumed by guilt over his de-gendered re-rendering of the war. I have warned some of the great historians whom I deeply admire that tackling their big im-portant subjects and then dedicating books to daughters is touching, but it would be of much more benefit to those beloved females if they actually *included* women in these his-torical tomes. By fully representing women in their prize-winning epics, historians would build a better future for all our children. I hope that what follows—morsels and slices culled from my own reading and research on women during the war—will serve as sharp, stinging rebukes to Burns, whose deaf ear on this topic has deprived us of the moving voices of women during the American Civil War who deserved so much better than he gave.

Women themselves regarded the war as an unfolding epic—one in which they would finally be allowed to play a leading role, as Septima Collis confessed: "During this four years' drama I was sometimes in the audience . . . once or twice upon the stage itself. When the curtain fell at last . . . they stamped their impression on my young life . . . they strength-ened me for undertaking for which I otherwise would have lacked nerve and endurance . . . and . . . gave me a fonder longing for the comforts of peace."[8]

Touching and sorrowful tales elicit our sympathy. The bereaved Mary Vaughn wrote in February 1863 from her plantation home, ironically named "Sunny Side":

> I do not think I am so much more sinful than others that he [God] should clutch my heart strings with his iron hand and tear them one by one asunder. First he took my dear grey-haired Father who had always been so dear and indulgent to me, but Charlie [her husband] was left to me, and well did he fill the place of Father and husband to me. Then little Willie [her infant son], still I did not murmur, but now, oh how, can I lift my voice in praise to Him who has taken from me the one hope of my life. I don't think I have had one thought apart from Charlie since we married. My every wish has been to try in some measure to return his devotion and untiring kindness. I cannot for the life of me realize my forlorn situation. He must come home yet. It cannot be true he has left me to suffer and endure alone. He always would shield me from everything like trouble and annoyance, how I can walk the dark future alone and unassisted by his strong arm of protection. I have but one wish and that is to die. You speak of my baby. Why, sister, will not God smite me there too? Will he not darken my young life to the utter most. I will crush back the love, welling up in the depths of my heart for the little one, so when God lays his chilling hand upon her limbs, it will not craze me. I have not read my bible since Charlie died. My tears and feelings seem frozen. I know, I feel but one thing, I am alone, utterly desolate.[9]

The suicidal widow renamed her baby girl "Charlie," and struggled on with her grief.

Burns focused on the experience of war as a military event, a choice which I can appreciate, especially as this enabled him to exploit fully the drama of a soldier's life and impending battles, bittersweet victories, and traumatic defeats. He mentions only in passing women who served as soldiers during the Civil War. Their numbers are in dispute, but North and South, black and white, we have evidence of disguised women performing with valor. Sarah Morgan wailed in her diary: "If I was a man. O if I was only a man. For two years that has been my only cry . . ."[10] while scores of young women went out and did something about it.

Rosetta Wakeman, who served with the 153rd Regiment New York State Volunteers as Private Edwin Wakeman, wrote home about her adventures: "Dear Mother and Father, Brothers and Sisters. . . . The first day of the fight our army got whip[ped] and we had to retreat back about ten miles. The next day the fight was renewed and the firing took place about eight o'Clock in the morning. There was a heavy Cannonading all day and a Sharp firing of infantry. I was not in the first day's fight but the next day I had to face the enemy bullets with my regiment. I was under fire about four hours and laid on the field of battle all night. There was three wounded in my Co. and one killed."[11] Wakeman participated in the Red River campaign where the commander issued an executive order that no women would accompany the troops, trying to rid the march of both family and camp followers. Little did he realize that not only Wakeman was serving in disguise, but we know Jeannie Hodges, an Irish immigrant, fought as Albert Cashier in this same campaign. Canadian-born Emma Edmonds enlisted in the 2nd Michigan as Private Franklin Thompson, and left us a memoir in which she thanked God in

1861 to be "permitted in this hour of my adopted country's need to express a tithe of gratitude which I feel toward the people of the Northern States."[12] After contracting malaria at the Battle of Fredericksburg she deserted, fearing her sex would be discovered. Solomon Newton, in the 10th Massachusetts, confided that "there was an orderly in one of our regiments and he and the Corporal always slept together. Well the other night the corporal had a baby for the corporal turned out to be a woman."[13]

We have much more documentation (especially through pension applications) of cases of women serving in the Union army than in the Confederate army. Yet white southern women donned uniforms for reasons as varied as their Yankee counterpart. One spectacular and unverified account is too good to be true: *The Woman in Battle: A Narrative of the Exploits, Adventures and Travels of Madame Loreta Janeta Velazquez* (1876), in which the author alleges to have been an enterprising and successful Confederate officer. She claimed she was a widow who assumed a male identity (Lieutenant Henry Buford), raised a cavalry company, spied for the Confederacy, served in battle, even romanced women in between twice being captured by the Union. (When her narrative appeared, Confederate General Jubal Early denounced the author's falsehoods and inconsistencies.)

Southerner Amy Clarke disguised herself to serve with her husband, and continued as a soldier even after he was killed at Shiloh. Clarke was eventually wounded and captured by Federals, who gave her a dress and sent her back behind Confederate lines. Less than two weeks before the end of the war, Mary Wright and Margaret Henry were captured and imprisoned; they claimed to have been fighting undetected for the Confederacy for years. Mary and Molly Bell, served under the names of Tom Parker and Bob Martin, but were accused by officers of being "common camp followers and . . . the means of demoralizing several hundred men."[14]

Burns was willing to shift from life under fire to the stench of sickness and death quite poignantly. The compelling tales of women in the wards would fill a full hour alone. Louisa May Alcott captured the harshness of a nurse's life when " . . . legless, armless occupants entering my ward admonished me that I was there to work, not to wonder or weep."[15] Former Charleston socialite Phoebe Pember complained of rats who "ate all the poultices applied during the night to the sick, and dragged away the pads stuffed with bran from under the arms and legs of the wounded."[16]

Pember faced even thornier problems when the wife of one of her patients overstayed her welcome, giving birth to a daughter on her husband's cot. Pember charitably tended to the newborn—who was named Phoebe by grateful parents. There were a good number of female offspring named after Clara Barton: she repeatedly challenged military and government dictates that banned women from the battlefield—making her a welcome nuisance during expeditions to battle sites, where Barton saved a good many men's lives by her heroic measures.[17] Juliet Hopkins, nicknamed "the Angel of the Confederacy," was wounded in the leg while nursing fallen soldiers at Seven Pines. She spent the rest of her life with a limp owing to this injury. Most women did not venture out onto the field, like the beloved Mother Bickerdyke, but waited for the wounded to come to them—and thousands upon thousands arrived.[18]

When some half-dead Alabama troops were deposited in the Confederate capital of Richmond, Alabama matron Fannie Beers rose to the occasion and, within a matter of hours, organized a hospital, enduring a baptism by fire: "Four of our sick died that night. I had never in my life witnessed a death-scene before, and had to fight hard to keep down the emotion which would have greatly impaired my usefulness."[19] She went on to serve as a hospital matron in four different hospitals. Kate Cumming of Mobile described a southern hospital scene in April 1862: "The men are lying all over the house on their blankets, just as they were brought from the battlefield. They are in the hall, on the gallery, and crowded into very small rooms. The foul air from this mass of human beings at first made me giddy and sick, but I soon got over it. We have to walk and, when we give the men anything, kneel in blood and water . . ."[20] Confederate nurse Selina Johnson remembered one patient following the Second Battle of Manassas/Bull Run: "The last few days he lived, the only way he could get any relief from terrible pain was for someone to clasp around the leg with both hands as near where it was cut off as they could and while clasping it tight, press the flesh down over the end of the bone. It was very hard work, so we nurses took turns."[21] Climbing aboard federal transports, one Sanitary Commission volunteer described the ghastly spectacle of Union suffering which greeted her: "Eighty-five fever cases, some in collapse, some with black stiff tongues which could not move for want of moisture; others muttering in low delirium. Sixty-three of our brave wounded and fifteen dead waiting for embalment [*sic*]."[22]

African American women had a special stake in the struggle, as they rightly perceived of the Civil War as a battle for black liberation: war, the dizzying carousel; and emancipation, the brass ring. Their moving roles in the Civil War are all but forgotten. Yes, Burns celebrates the remarkable Harriet

Tubman, but the millions more excluded demand more serious attention. Many slave women found war was sheer hell, as the Missouri wife who wrote her husband: "They are treating me worse and worse every day. Our child cries for you. Send me some money as soon as you can for me and my child are almost naked."[23] In Louisiana a white commander of a black regiment complained:

> A practice had largely obtained among owners of female slaves to secure for them free men as husbands—some of these husbands are in my reg't. When it appeared that they had entered the service, they were forbidden by the owners of their wives the permission and privileges before accorded them, and such treatment is practiced upon their wives and children as to exasperate them as has in some instances tended to breaches of the peace.[24]

Spottswood Rice wrote to his daughters left behind in rural Missouri: " . . . my respects is worn out and have no sympathy for Slaveholders. And as for her cristianantty [the mistress] I expect the Devil has such in hell. You tell her from me that she is the frist chirstian that I ever hard say that aman could Steal his own child especially out of human bondage . . ." His bravado stemmed from that fact that even as he lay in a hospital bed in St. Louis, he planned their rescue: "Be assured that I will have you if it cost me my life on the 28th of the mounth. 8 hundred White and 8 hundred blacke solders expects to start up the rivore to Glasgow . . . when they Come I expect to be with them and expect to get you both in return. Dont be uneasy my children."[25]

Desperate circumstances caused drastic results. One Kentucky woman attempted to spirit her children away, only to be accosted by her master's son-in-law "who told me that if I did not go back with him he would shoot me. He drew a pistol on me as he made this threat. I could offer no resistance as he constantly kept the pistol pointed at me."[26] She was forced to return home at gun point, while the white man kidnapped her seven-year-old as hostage.

The depletion of *adult* labor increased the burdens on slave children. Eliza Scantling, fifteen in 1865, remembered she "plowed a mule an' a wild un at dat. Sometimes me hands get so cold I jes' cry."[27] For slave children the prospect of an invading enemy was confusing and, at times, terrifying. Mittie Freeman, at ten, hid in a tree when the first bluecoats arrived. As slave men fled the plantations, many left wives and children behind. During wartime, thousands were fatherless and hundreds were orphaned. Amie Lumpkin of South Carolina recalled her wartime loss: "My daddy go 'way to de war 'bout dis time, and my mammy and me stay in our cabin alone. She cry and wonder where he be, if he is well or he be killed, and one day we hear he is dead. My mammy, too, pass in a short time."[28]

Sacrifice was equally onerous for black and white in the Confederacy. White survivors of the war developed legends into an art form, depicting brutish humiliations, ghastly deprivations, and enormous forfeiture to barbaric Yankees, who wielded absolute and corrupt power within the occupied South.

After Yankees burned her home, Rebecca Ridley lived in the cookhouse of her former plantation—Fair Mont, outside Murfreesborough, Tenn. Following a battle, Ridley reported: "The ground has been covered with snow and ice—freezing our poor unprotected soldiers—some of them I understand are barefooted, none have tents—or a sufficiency of blankets and all have to depend on the country for subsistence—poor fellows, how my heart bleeds for them. They come in at the houses to warm, and get something to eat, and some of our citizens who pretend to be very Southern grudge them the food they eat—say they will be eat out."[29] Patriot Katie Miller reported to her aunt, "I told ma when *provisions* got so low that she couldn't feed a passing soldier to let me know every-time one comes and I would go minus one meal for him."[30]

Louisa Henry fled from her plantation into the woods, but as the wife of a Rebel quartermaster, she was sought out by the bluecoats and confided: "I was in *mortal* terror all the time they were here, the children were clinging to my skirts, crying fit to break their hearts which prevented some of the brutal set from *burning the house*, so they told the negroes. . . ."[31] The savagery of torching prompted Henrietta Lee to write directly to Union commander General David Hunter: "Yes-terday your underling, Captain Martindale, of the First New York Cavalry, executed your infamous order and burned my house . . . the dwelling and every outbuilding, seven in number, with their contents being burned. I, therefore, a help-less woman whom you have cruelly wronged, address you, a Major General of the United States Army, and demand [to know] why this was done . . . Hyena-like, you have torn my heart to pieces! For all hallowed memories clustered around that homestead; and demon-like, you have done it without even the pretext of revenge . . . Your name will stand on history's pages as the Hunter of weak women, and inno-cent children: the Hunter to destroy defenseless villages and beautiful homes—to torture afresh the agonized hearts of widows."[32] Confederate matrons embraced a cult of sacrifice, one of the most compelling chapters of wartime drama. Perhaps Burns thought *Gone With the Wind* had covered the topic adequately, but he did not stint on Gettysburg and battle-related issues, while the homefronts, North and South, were slighted.

Further, his focus on military campaigns skimped those issues involving women and civilians when they *were* germane: for example, during the infamous Sherman's March, and again, during the siege of Vicksburg, when hundreds of trapped civilians lived in caves, fighting off starvation and the Yankee assault. This wartime heroism has taken on legendary proportion, with good reason. The memoir of Mary Ann Loughborough provides wrenching detail: a songbird turned into soup for her child, a slave tossing a live shell out of a cave. Bombardments kept everyone on alert and daily life was precarious at best and, upon occasion, deadly. Loughborough described a little girl who played outside, but "on returning, an explosion sounded near her—one wild scream and she ran into her mother's presence, sinking like a wounded dove, the life blood flowing over the light summer dress in crimson ripples from a death wound in her side caused by the shell fragment."[33] Burns described soldiers catching rats for food, but what of those without uniforms who died in battle as well?

Like the ranting colleagues I disparage, I could go on, and on and on. But I would like to close with the story of one black woman whom Burns mentioned and quoted, but someone whose story he failed to finish in his final episode: Susie King Taylor.[34]

Taylor was born on a Georgia plantation in 1848, the first child of a slave mother named Baker. Her grandmother was born in 1820, the granddaughter of an African slave brought to Georgia during the 1730s. Taylor went to live with her grandmother in Savannah, escaping the plantation when she was just a young girl. During her years in Savannah, she was fortunate to have white playmates willing to teach her to read and write, in that offering instruction to a slave was against the law.

One of her tutors abandoned her to serve with the Savannah Volunteer Guards when the war broke out in 1861. Taylor vividly recalled the shelling of Fort Pulaski, which prompted her return to the countryside to be with her mother: "I remember what a roar and din the guns made. They jarred the earth for miles."[35] When federals captured the fort, Taylor was ferried behind Union lines, onto St. Simon's Island. Because she could read and write, white Union officers drafted her, at the age of fourteen, to teach freed slaves. She married a black soldier, a sergeant with the first South Carolina Volunteers, and subsequently served alongside her husband as a nurse and laundress for the troops.

Taylor practiced other skills as well and confided: "I learned to handle a musket very well while in the regiment, and could shoot straight and often hit the target."[36] When Clara Barton came to the sea islands, she worked alongside her. Taylor remained with her regiment through February 1865.

After the war Taylor resettled in Savannah and opened a school. But when her husband died in 1866, she faced an uncertain and unsettling future, as she was left "soon to welcome a little stranger alone." Pregnant and widowed, she struggled to survive. By 1868 Taylor had to close her school, and in 1872 she left her child with her parents and took a job as a domestic for a wealthy Savannah family. Unlike most women of her race and class, she did not spend the rest of her years in this role, slavery's legacy. Rather, Taylor secured a job in Boston, then remarried, and embarked on a career as a club-woman and civic activist. In 1902 she published *Reminiscences of My Life in Camp with the 33rd United States Colored Troops, Late 1st S.C. Volunteers*, a remarkable chronicle of her life told with poignant insight.

Despite the great rarity of her account, Taylor made a dramatic point near the end of her memoir, which speaks to us across the generations:

> There are many people who do not know what some of the colored women did during the war. There were hundreds of them who assisted the Union soldiers by hiding them and helping them to escape. Many were punished for taking food to the prison stockades for the prisoners . . . Others assisted in various ways the Union army. **These things should be kept in history before the people. There has never been a greater war in the United States than the one of 1861, where so many lives were lost,—not men alone but noble women as well** [emphasis added].[37]

5

Lincoln and Gettysburg:
The Hero and the Heroic Place

GABOR S. BORITT

*F*OR A LONG TIME IN THE Gettysburg National Military Park a solitary stone wall left standing from a destroyed barn evoked, better than anything else, the American Civil War. Purists, some might say the small-minded, objected vehemently, wanting it pulled down. After all, George Rose's barn did not start to crumble until 1934, long after the weary troops of generals Robert E. Lee and George Gordon Meade had left forever. But the tall wall stood there, amidst lush green and amidst white snow, year after year, decade following decade. Experts continued to grumble until at last, in 1985, a windstorm blew it down. The strong Pennsylvania stones that had for so long withstood the wind and weather and expert criticism make a fine metaphor for one of the important achievements by the students of the great American tragedy and triumph: the PBS documentary series *The Civil War,* by Ken Burns, Ric Burns, and Geoffrey C. Ward.

The eleven-hour-long masterpiece is a major contribution to how Americans perceive this central event of their history—indeed war in general. It follows in the tradition of brilliant filmmaking which began with D.W. Griffith's *The Birth of a Nation* in 1915. Woodrow Wilson described that work as "writing history with lightning," but better testimony to its terrifying power came with the black men lynched in the film's wake and the rebirth of the KKK.[1] Nearly a quarter of a century later David O. Selznick's 1939 *Gone With the Wind* demonstrated anew, if in a more subtle and less malignant manner, that cinema about the Civil War continued to matter. Its long reign as the premier film on the War, and the premier romanticization of the "world the slaveholders made," may have come to an end with the PBS documentary. The series was seen, when first shown in the fall of 1990, at least in some part by close to 40 million people.[2] Repeated runs on television and simultaneous release on video continue to add untold millions to its viewing audience. Its influence remains to be gauged, but George Bush and Colin Powell in Washington, and Norman Schwarzkopf in Saudi Arabia, provided immediate and poignant illustrations as they watched the film hour after hour with its deeply disturbing emphasis on casualties—even as they led the country into war with Iraq.[3] The documentary reinforced their insistence on a strategy that tried to minimize American casualties. The re-creation of Civil War history still matters in the making of new American history.

This film is a close kin of literature. Words count for nearly as much in it as images and sounds. The team of filmmakers have both the ears and the eyes of poets. They turn dull black and white photos into haunting images full of life. The pictures hold us captive. They make us choke up. And so do the words.

More than 800 quotations and a fine connecting narrative frame the images. In a nation uninterested in history, and for a visually oriented generation uninterested in reading, the film invokes the power of the native tongue. Thanks to it millions heard American words from a time when the American language reached perhaps its high-water mark for eloquence. The words may come from a Mary Boykin Chesnut, a Walt Whitman, an Abraham Lincoln, or a Frederick Douglass. Or they may come, even more often, from people long forgotten. We see men with guns. Soldiers charge. "They seemed to melt like snow coming down on warm ground"—the words of an unnamed officer. The Burns brothers, at least, knew little about the War when embarking on this work, and their fresh-eyed innocence, combined with Ward's seasoned talent, captured an essence that eluded experts.

Their perspective is national. Claims of southern exceptionalism are not granted. A separate southern white belief system is given even shorter shrift than its northern counterpart. Not surprisingly, even as the documentary first aired, accusations of anti-southern prejudice, meaning anti-southern-white prejudice, started to fly, a charge nicely summed up by the *Southern Partisan* cartoon showing General Grant leaning against a giant television screen carrying the words "PBS: The Civil War" and with the caption adding: "Brought to you by U.S. Grant."[4]

Yet the film tries hard to be fair-minded. If we take Gettysburg as a test case, for example, the above becomes obvious even if a northern colonel is made into the battle's hero. One can understand why some southerners would dislike Robert E. Lee's demotion but, after all, he lost that battle and his brilliance is amply recognized elsewhere.

Others could similarly bristle at Andersonville's being made the symbol of atrocity. We are shown photos of the prison's survivors. They match the survivors of Nazi death camps, and we know that the Confederate commandant was German-born. Anger, however, is directed at the wrong place, even if most northern prisoners of war camps were also abominations. The Burns brothers, whose Confederate ancestors incidentally outnumbered their Union ones, and who made Shelby Foote, this wonderful Memphis voice, the film's star, intend no injustice. It is true that the North won the War, many Yankee values became dominant American values, and the Burns brothers and Ward are Americans. But their Andersonville is not so much a Rebel crime as it is an American crime. It represents all the prisons and all the victims of the Civil War, indeed all victims of the horrors of war at all times. And the filmmakers' love of both southerners and northerners, blacks and whites shines through everywhere. Much of this nation is ready for such an approach to the past.[5]

This is not to deny that as history the documentary is open to questions. Most important, it makes the Civil War the central event of U.S. history—in the words of novelist-historian Foote, "the cross roads of our being," America's defining moment. I, too, feel the attraction of such a faith. But scholars who see the story of humanity in terms of long-range processes should be very uncomfortable with it. Even within the four-year focus, these and other historians, too, would want a systematic look at the home front, women, indeed social history in general. Professors would want a more accurate reflection of the present state of academic interpretation/turf wars. The same might be said for the less fashionable fields of the moment: religious, diplomatic, cultural, intellectual, constitutional, and economic history. The past as the story of individuals, as history on film almost always is, receives much less than the universal assent of academia. How well does the documentary absorb the general scholarly knowledge of the era? For example, did any factors besides slavery deserve close attention in the coming of the War? How well is that one all-important factor handled? But on these and other matters scholars themselves disagree. These filmmakers have earned the right to their own interpretations.

What historians would call "methodology" combines here music and sound effects, text read by forty fine voices, and visual materials, primarily old photographs supplemented by virtuoso cinematography. Yet even as dead photos are endowed with unprecedented poetic brilliance, image and text do not always match. The rare expert familiar with the visuals receives repeated jolts. A voice speaks of a college in Gettysburg, the photo shows the Lutheran Seminary of the now historic town. Voice: Chancellorsville; photo: Wilderness. Voice: Mrs. Chesnut; photo: unknown woman. And so on. How much mismatching is demanded or justified by art? We would rebel if Lincoln's words were attributed to Grant, or Sullivan Ballou's to another soldier. Yet photographs are as much historical documents as speeches or letters. For historians who have made great strides in turning photos into specific historical documents (rather than works of art or generic props), *The Civil War* can represent a bitter setback. At a minimum the film needed a strong disclaimer.[6]

Yet the historian also grows quickly aware of his craft's limitations in taking such a critique far. When the Lincoln of 1864 is discussed but that of 1862 is shown I am disgruntled as a scholar but wonder about the possible artistic rationale that I may not understand. How to balance the historical loss against an artistic gain? In places the mismatching is obviously intentional, obvious to nearly all, and quite welcome. The narrator speaks of Robert E. Lee, a rather recognizable figure, carefully observing his early counterpart George B. McClellan. The image shown is that of an unknown officer looking through a telescope. Good and simple. Respectable ideology accounts for Confederate pickets appearing to the accompaniment of the "Battle Hymn of the Republic." Similarly, but with even greater intelligence, "Marching Through Georgia" fills our ears—the rousing Yankee tune well hated by white southerners at the time, and beyond—as Sherman's men march. But then the music continues when pitiful scenes of devastation cloud the screen. This would be incongruous with the tone of the documentary but for one fact: the music is slowed down; the march becomes a lament.

Still, out-of-place photographs disturb one of the most striking elements of the film: the many photos of the dead, including at Gettysburg. Ken Burns is not so much obsessed with death as he is its friend, one who has made utter peace with it. He often teaches us with photos which the Civil War era public never saw. Mutilated bodies, with parts blown away; men grievously wounded; amputees; people soon to be corpses; a pile of limbs. These give an anti-war ethos to the film which helps explain its warm embrace by post-Vietnam America. The contradiction between being *against* war and *for* its results—in this case black freedom an emphasis that also accounts for the success of the series—is no more resolved by the film than by the scholars who are equally the products of the anti-war and civil rights era of the sixties and after.

The contradiction above springs from "the hearts and minds" of the creators of the film. Others result from the presence of historians with contrasting interpretations, and perhaps in part from editing. The documentary pictures Lincoln as the emancipator. But the Columbia University historian Barbara Fields dissents, giving most of the credit for black freedom to African-Americans themselves. "It is not true," she claims, that it was "impossible" for Lincoln "to look any higher." The viewer can make up her or his own mind about the truth of history.

The soundtrack provides a rich variety of regional dialects. Even a few effete European voices are heard, sometimes to criticize the North with disdain. Sorely missing, however, are the *sounds* of the immigrants who made up perhaps 10 percent of the Confederate and 25 percent of the Union armies. The Germans, the Irish, and so many others. When German-born General Carl Schurz speaks no old-country accent appears. African-Americans are accorded a deservedly large role in the northern victory (even as their important if coerced contribution to the southern home front is ignored as is their brave sabotage of that front). The immigrants, however, remain unheard at Gettysburg, and at every other battlefield. Burns thus unwittingly re-creates some of the ethnic tensions of the 1860s, and of our own times.

Many of the finest scholars of the Civil War period served as advisers to the film, a few appeared in it, and the work of others, too, is borrowed freely. Finding myself being quoted verbatim, in part one, without attribution—when the film speaks of Lincoln and "the right to rise"—I remembered Cyrano's retort when told that Molière stole from him: "Bah—he showed good taste."[7] A film cannot have footnotes after all and students of the Civil War surely owe as much to Burns and company as vice versa. Yet what he and his co-workers badly needed was a team of graduate-student fact-checkers, or the like, to comb *carefully* through all of the footage for errors—and most of all a military historian since so much of the film targets the War on land, though not that on the water. Gettysburg, July 1–3, 1863, illustrates the point. So does the rendering of the Lincoln image.

Gettysburg, day one. "The greatest battle ever fought on the North American continent began as a clash over shoes." Folktale. The series uses these masterfully but ahistorically. "The South came in from the North that day and the North came in from the South." A fine sentence that stresses paradox. But the Confederates came in from the west, then the north. Mundane facts at times lose out to the well-turned phrase or the enticing image. "Compared to what was coming, the first day had been a skirmish." Without going into arguments over exact numbers of troops and precise times—a veritable labyrinth—it is clear that the first day, producing close to one-third of the three days' casualties, was anything but a skirmish. It foreshadowed what was to come.

Day one also illustrates the impossibility of providing on film the detailed scrutiny, the sophistication of interpretation that we demand from books. Toward the evening of July 1, General Lee ordered the commander of his Second Corps, Richard S. Ewell, to take Culp's Hill, "if practicable." Ewell did not attack, and the Hill remained an anchor of the Union line for the rest of the battle. Folklore, and historical writers who tried to absolve Lee from responsibility for Gettysburg, made Ewell one of its great scapegoats. Many a Civil War buff is certain that had the aggressive Stonewall Jackson not died a few weeks earlier at Chancellorsville, Gettysburg might have been a different story. The film devotes but a moment to the topic, simply and subtly blaming Ewell. We get no intimation that historians themselves disagree, that it is quite possible to make a case for the bold-headed Lieutenant General from Virginia.[8]

One heroic episode dominates day two: the defense of Little Round Top by Joshua Chamberlain and the 20th Maine. Such a twist provides literal testimony (in addition to the necessities of filmmaking) to the adage that the pen is mightier than the sword. A professor of rhetoric from Bowdoin College, Chamberlain wrote excellent after-battle reports and memoirs. Not surprisingly, his 20th Maine eventually attracted a fine regimental historian and, most important, in 1975, Michael Shaara, whose novel about the battle, *The Killer Angels*, won the Pulitzer Prize. Shaara made the professor-colonel from Maine into a folk hero. The film thus reflects sensitively the evolving mythology of the battle.[9]

PBS's *The Civil War* has been followed by Ron Maxwell's *Gettysburg*, the translation of *The Killer Angels* into an epic film (as well as television series and best-selling video). The earlier triumph helped make Maxwell's film possible. And the latter, faithful to Shaara's original conception, and enhanced by a stellar performance by actor Jeff Daniels as Joshua Chamberlain, made the soldier from Maine into *the* hero of Gettysburg for the interested general public. But in film history, the PBS series signaled the turning point.

Chamberlain indeed was an important figure in the battle. Little Round Top protected the Union left flank and rear, and the man from Maine played a remarkable role in saving it. But the other units that helped defend Little Round Top, and much of the rest of the action on the rest of the battlefield that made day two at Gettysburg a crucial stalemate, disappear from "*The Civil War*" almost entirely.

Day three is Pickett's Charge. The seven-hour struggle for Culp's Hill is lost. Chronology is upended for the sake of drama. The visual images at times do not match the spoken words and when they do they can still give a false impression. For example Lewis Armistead, who breaches the Federal center, is shown on horseback in the romantic painting of Paul Philippoteaux that now hangs in the Cyclorama of the Gettysburg National Military Park. Of course the Virginian marched and ran, like the other rebs, because a man on horseback could not have survived on the slopes of Cemetery Ridge. One wonders whether discomfort with military matters produces gaffes that turn "aim low" into the soundtrack's "aim slow," or is Garrison Keillor misreading the text and nobody knows enough to catch the error? Is this why the Taneytown Road becomes the Tarreytown Road? The inconsequential and the historically forgivable shade into the substantive until the battle becomes little more than the saga of Chamberlain and Pickett's Charge.[10]

After the battle the Union commander, George G. Meade, loses the "opportunity to destroy the Army of Northern Virginia." If anything might be said for Meade it remains unsaid. All along the complex becomes simple. The battle after all is fought in the film to relieve the siege of Vicksburg and no more; and fought at Gettysburg because of a search for nonexistent shoes.

Then there are the misquotations. For example, Shelby Foote butchers—well, paraphrases is more charitable—William Faulkner's memorable lines: "For every Southern boy fourteen years old, not once, but whenever he wants it, there is the instant when it's still not yet two o'clock on that July afternoon in 1863. . . ." That Everyboy, indeed as Faulkner admits, that Everyman can forever hope, "*This time.* Maybe this time. . . ." Pickett's Charge may turn out differently. Edwin Bearss, another unforgettable character in the documentary, and in life, does the same garbling with British statesman William Gladstone's words: "Jefferson Davis and other leaders of the South have made an army; they are making, it appears, a navy; and they have made what is more than either—they have made a nation." Lincoln's biographer, and at times his alter ego in the film, Stephen Oates, does rather better. The words of the Second Inaugural—"Both read the same Bible, and pray to the same God; and each invokes His aid against the other"—becomes "We both pray to the same God. We both invoked Him. We both said we were on His side." But this is still not Lincoln and the tenses are mixed to boot. Of course, Oates, Foote, Bearss, and the others are all on candid camera. What they do is what professors do in their classrooms, what we all who love and talk history do in our everyday conversations.[12]

And so I am about to get off my professional high horse. After spitting out what to many must seem malicious quibbles (who cares whether General Armistead rode a horse?) it is joyous to shout that the Gettysburg segment, like the film as a whole, is miraculously good art. Chamberlain, and Pickett, and Burns *do* make the battle come alive. And more. When the sunlight hits the cannon through the tree tops on the ridge we know it is early afternoon, July 3, time for the Charge. The Burns brothers filmed on the right day at the right time. The rains come because they had in 1863. The birds sing because they are native to the ground.

We see in the background a 104-year-old black woman, Daisy Turner, eyes shut, reciting war poetry. Her father was a slave, escaped, joined the U.S. Army, returned south and shot his former overseer. We want to believe. Even the expert forgets to analyze the words, the photographs, the paintings. They belong, our senses tell us. This beautiful African-

American woman starts the Gettysburg segment of the film. When the actual battle begins she is there; she is there, too, in the middle of the fight; and the battle ends with her sad poetry. And so the film finds a wonderful, luminous solution to a vexing problem historians have failed to solve before: the absence of blacks from the most famous, perhaps most important battle of a war in which they had a central role. God bless Daisy Turner and those who had the inspiration to bring her to Gettysburg.[13]

One verse of Turner's lament for the dead comes right after what appears to be the death of a Confederate soldier, Albert Bachelor. It adds a wonderful de-ideologizing human face to the battle—one that no doubt irritates others with different sensibilities. But for Burns the dead earned our mourning, whichever side they had fought on. Earlier this soldier's father wrote: "It gives me great relief of mind to hear that you and your dear brothers were still in the land of the living." Then he gets the news from another son that Albert is shot through the leg and the left eye. The brother carries him to a field hospital and writes home: "Dropping a tear of grief upon his bleeding face, I bade him goodbye." The accompanying images wrench one's heart, too, and the viewer says goodby to the young man who had hardly lived. But then we get a final letter: "My Dear Father: It has pleased the God of Battles that I should number among the many wounded. . . . Through his infinite kindness and mercy I am permitted to inform you that I have recovered . . . Your devoted son. Albert Bachelor." One is choked by gratitude. Such mercies by the filmmakers make the carnage a little more bearable.

When July 3 is described as "the most crucial day of the entire war," intellectuals in general and historians in particular might cringe. We like to avert our eyes from war. We often say that Lincoln's words in the November after the battle were the important facts and made Gettysburg into the central heroic place of the Civil War. But the film emphasizes the battle and makes the "Gettysburg Address," however brilliantly portrayed, an epilogue. This fits well the documentary's overall approach that puts war, as that word is commonly understood to mean soldiers and fighting, at the heart of *The Civil War*. That is as it should be.

Daisy Turner, Albert Bachelor, Pickett, they all belong to Gettysburg. So do the sounds of battle, muffled in the background: marching feet, horses' hoofs, neighing, wagons, artillery rumbling, something like a Rebel yell, guns fired, night noises, insects buzzing, birds, a piano. They take away your breath. They put tears in your eyes. They underscore the historical insights. Shelby Foote: "Gettysburg was the price the South paid for having Robert E. Lee. That was the mistake he made. The mistake of all mistakes." We know that we could not find 13,000 men in the Western world today for Pickett, to charge against those Yankee guns. Why did the soldiers fight? *Why* did they go up Cemetery Ridge? Then we hear a rebel officer urging his men, attacking south against the insurmountable northern breastworks: "Home, boys, home! Remember, *home* is over beyond those hills!" We almost understand.

If Gettysburg is the only battle to receive sustained attention, Lincoln is the only political leader to do so. A little of what makes Chamberlain the victorious knight of the battle, deserving a lion's share of our attention, makes Gettysburg the central event of the war, and Lincoln the central figure. The heroic place and the greatest of heroes. A narrative story on film cannot easily avoid making events its focus and individuals its heroes. And it must have heroes in most cases. Given a good part of academia's de-emphasis of the role of individuals in history, given its growing aversion to heroic figures, *The Civil War* provides a welcome antidote. In any case, if I am right in believing that the personalization of history could not be avoided, it is altogether fitting for the film to make the North's, indeed the country's, most eloquent voice and most effective instrument into its symbol. And so Lincoln moves to the forefront of the historical process where most Americans believe he belongs—not to mention those on the rest of the globe that know something about American history.[14]

The small errors of Gettysburg are repeated with Lincoln, too. To illustrate, he is introduced as a prophet in the Prologue of the film. "Whence shall we expect the approach of danger?" he asks in 1838. "Shall some trans-Atlantic giant step the earth and crush us at a blow? Never. All the armies of Europe and Asia could not by force take a drink from the Ohio River or make a track on the Blue Ridge in the trial of a thousand years. If destruction be our lot, we must ourselves be its author and finisher. As a nation of freemen, we will live forever or die by suicide." So Lincoln seems to foretell the future. But a look at the context of his words tells something else: mob violence beset the America of the 1830s, including Lincoln's Illinois, and he spoke up against it firmly, with youthful bravado and eloquence. However, as late as the start of 1861 he refused to believe that appeals to arms would be answered in United States. "There will be no war," he repeated incessantly.[15]

Not only did Lincoln fail to see the coming of the Civil War, like so much of the country, but the filmmakers also paraphrase him while the viewer is under the impression that she/he is listening to Lincoln's exact words. I see no easy solution to the inability of film to identify elliptical additions to quotations, but unnecessary substitutions suggest carelessness.[16]

Lincoln's words quoted above are also misdated to 1837. Similarly, the start of his political career in the Illinois legislature is put to age 24 though he reached that body late in his 25th year. At the other end of his life John Wilkes Booth assassinates him at age 54; in actuality he turned 56 before the bullet struck him. Trivia but bothersome.

Booth in turn is introduced via a photograph of a militia unit, the Richmond Greys. But the somewhat Booth-looking figure in the picture is not the future assassin.[17] Happily and more important, Booth is allowed to hover with great effect around the edges of the story until at last he takes center stage. Then the documentary's creators resolutely avoid the plethora of crackpot conspiracy theories that the public loves.

And so let me get around to my basic point. Quibbles notwithstanding, I like very much the Lincoln created by the documentary. A film that relies so much on words could hardly do better than make the American West's master of words its central political figure. Carelessness cannot be excused, but Ward and company selected a brilliant, meaningful array of Lincoln quotations. The jokes from the President are funny though, of course, less readily authenticable. Actor Sam Waterston gives a truly fine voice to Lincoln's words (though not as fine as the very believable, high-pitched, old Appalachian sound he used for the 1993 Broadway revival of *Abe Lincoln of Illinois*).[18] And historian Oates and former Congressman James Symington provide often thoughtful commentary on the President.

Still, many historians will object to this Lincoln portrait as uncritical. Whether we see Lincoln as the political leader, commander-in-chief, or even as husband and father, he is the hero. But America's increasingly nihilistic culture badly needs heroes and heroic places. Perhaps only with a single issue, slavery, do we get a multidimensional, even contradictory look from the documentary. At times Lincoln is made to appear more anti-slavery than he was; at times less. But that aspect is explored in another part of this book.

I am painfully aware that the kind of critique that this chapter, and perhaps this volume, provides befits a book more than a film. To look mostly at text, the words spoken, seems grossly unfair. I wish I could conjure the film unto these pages—the evocation of the Gettysburg Address, for example. But that cannot be. So a mundane summary must do.

The segment begins with the fine narrator, historian David McCullough, intoning the by now famous lines: "The Civil War was fought in ten thousand places. . . ." Names roll on, from unknown spots of the map to Gettysburg. Our eyes fasten on a modern nature-shot in color, and in the background Jay Ungar and Molly Mason play the folktune "Shenandoah" on nineteenth-century folk instruments. Then an interview, James Symington: "I think if I had my choice of all the moments to be present at in the war period, it would be at Gettysburg, during Lincoln's delivery. . . ."

Everett's speech is noted, his face, an old program for the ceremonies, and photos of the crowds of 1863. Lincoln stands up and a photographer gets ready with his apparatus. Before he can open his shutter the speech is done.

But other pictures were taken, and the camera artfully highlights their details. Now the interview, Shelby Foote:

Lincoln "felt that he had failed." Then two contemporary comments. The *Chicago Times*: "The cheek of every American must tingle with shame as he reads the silly, flat, dish-watery utterances . . ."; and Everett's praise to the President: "I should be glad if I could flatter myself that I came as near to the central idea of the occasion, in two hours, as you did in five minutes." Next we see a contemporary photo of the gate of the Gettysburg Cemetery. The camera slowly moves in on the anonymous figure in the background, just inside the gate, whom the millions who have seen that picture surely have taken no notice of before. Then the address.

"The Ashokan Farewell" begins, Ungar's unforgettable lament that Burns made the theme music of the film and into a nationally loved anthem. Sam Waterston interprets the words. We see photos of the Civil War dead; film clips of the old men of the last soldiers' reunion in Gettysburg, 1938; then a Gardner photo of Lincoln. It has never been done better.

Of course the paragraphs above amount to only sickly reportage. And the scholar can take the Gettysburg Address segment apart, too. It contains errors of fact, perhaps errors of interpretation. But the beauty of the film silences the critical voice.

The rapid pace of change in modern life makes it all but certain that in time *The Civil War* will be supplanted by other works of history and art that will also reach millions in the United States and, perhaps, around the globe. What might be the medium of such histories stretches the boundaries of our imaginations. We are left at sea—just as the work of Ken Burns and company may have been beyond the horizon of a James Ford Rhodes (1848–1927), though not that of an Allan Nevins (1890–1971), two historians whose epic affirmations of the American nation might be seen as the precious heritage of our filmmakers. It is an act of faith to say this, but as the American people approach a new century and a new millennium, as they embrace, one hopes, ever more comfortably, even fondly, their diversity, they badly need that heritage.

It is preposterous to compare great works that outlasted millennia with one created during the past few years. Still, as one lovingly contemplates *The Civil War* it conjures up the *Iliad*, the story of a war from the perspective of the winner, the perspective that mostly survives. Homer, of course, is not very good history. Nor are the works that have made history live over the ages, the Bible, *Beowulf*, the *Shah-nama*, the *Mahabharata*, the *Three Kingdoms, Heiki Monogatari, Hiawatha*, and *Shaka*. None are good history. By the strict and, for the literate general public, often deadening standards of academe, neither is this work of Ken Burns, Geoffrey Ward, and Ric Burns. That it is touched by the fire of great gifts, however, cannot be denied. It challenges our understanding of what history is.

6

Ken Burns and the Romance of Reunion

ERIC FONER

*I*N THE NINTH AND FINAL episode of *The Civil War*, filmmaker Ken Burns faced a daunting challenge: how to bring the war's story to a close, describe its immediate aftermath, and assess its legacy for American history. If the episode is, as I believe, the weakest of the series, it is only fair to note that Burns is not the first historian to be bedeviled by this challenge and ultimately defeated by it. Some, for instance, simply conclude their account with the surrender of Lee and the assassination of Lincoln, as though after April 1865 nothing happened. Others recognize that one cannot appraise the war's meaning or consider whether its accomplishments justified the enormous loss of life without examining the years immediately following the Confederacy's defeat and the long road to reunion that stretched into the new century. The postwar years, however, lack both the drama of the battlefield and the war's easily recognizable cast of characters. Nor do they end, even for the winning side, in a blaze of glory.

The problem of "closure" is especially acute in a television series intended for a mass public. Americans have rarely expressed much interest in the Reconstruction years that followed the Civil War, probably the most controversial and misunderstood era in our nation's past. A survey of high school seniors recently conducted by the *Los Angeles Times* reported that fewer were able to identify Reconstruction than any other event or period of American history. "What the American public always wants," William Dean Howells once remarked, "is a tragedy with a happy ending."[1] History, alas, seldom provides unambiguously festive conclusions, nor do wars neatly settle profound political and ideological issues. The more closely one looks at the aftermath of the Civil War, the more disturbing the consequences are likely to be.

Burns appears to have found the war itself far more "digestible" than either its origins or consequences. Just as the opening installment raced through the prewar decades in order to get to the battles (leaving viewers with no coherent sense of what caused the conflict in the first place), so its conclusion lingers on the events of April and May 1865—the final surrender of Confederate armies, the assassination and funeral of Abraham Lincoln—getting to the postwar era only when the episode is already half over. Then it rushes through Reconstruction to dwell at length on reunions of Union and Confederate veterans, especially the famous gathering at Gettysburg in 1913 that marked the fiftieth anniversary of the Civil War's biggest battle. From the opening remarks of the historians Barbara Fields and Shelby Foote that the Civil War created the United States, to the final acknowledgment by the veterans that each side had fought nobly for its own ideals, Burns's message is clear: the chief legacy of the war was the survival and consolidation of the nation state, and that of the postwar era the re-establishment of a sense of national unity. As the historian David Blight has remarked, this combination of nostalgia and national celebration is a "most appealing" legacy, which manages to ignore all those issues that raise troubling questions about American society today.[2]

Even on Burns's favored terrain, military history, the account of the war's ending is remarkably impoverished. There is no reflection on the war as a whole and its place in the history of warfare, no effort to assess the overall impact of industrial technology on the conflict or to sum up the strategy that finally led to northern victory. Indeed, Burns fails even to explain *why* the North triumphed on the battlefield, except to note the fact that it possessed superior resources—hardly a guarantee of victory, as history has so often demonstrated. Once he moves to the war's broader implications and consequences, he has even less to say. Issues central to the Civil War and of obvious contemporary relevance—self-determination, political democracy, race relations, the balance between force and consent in maintaining political authority—are never addressed. The abolition of slavery is never mentioned explicitly as part of the war's meaning, while the unfulfilled promise of emancipation is all but ignored as central to its aftermath. Nor is it ever suggested that the abandonment of the nation's postwar commitment to equal rights for the former slaves was the basis on which former (white) antagonists could unite in the romance of reunion. In choosing to stress the preservation of the American nation state as the war's most enduring consequence, Burns privileges a merely national concern over the great human drama of emancipation. The result is a strangely parochial vision of the Civil War and its aftermath, and a missed opportunity to stimulate thinking about political and moral questions still central to our society.

In choosing reunion as the theme and the veteran as the emblem of this last episode, Burns magnifies weaknesses common to the series as a whole while relinquishing the strengths of earlier segments, especially the rich feeling for how individuals exist in specific times and places. The second half of the episode abandons any sense of chronology or historical context. Burns makes no attempt to convey the state of the nation at war's end in 1865, and no explanation is offered for the failure to guarantee the equal rights of the former slaves. The photographs and newsreel footage recording the veterans' reunions are presented without regard to time or place, and even on occasion without proper identification—as though the events themselves took place in a historical vacuum. A mention of the Ku Klux Klan during Reconstruction, for example, is illustrated by a famous picture of Klansmen parading through the streets of Washington in the 1920s, and photos of reunions from two generations afterwards accompany narration about 1865. After the detailed attention to historical chronology in previous episodes, where battles were examined day by day, even hour by hour, such complete disregard for historical sequence (to say nothing of historical causation) is profoundly disturbing.

Anecdotes and snippets of information about individual lives dominate the entire series, reducing, in good television fashion, the political to the personal. In the final episode, however, bereft of the rich texture of earlier segments, these elements lose all historical meaning, not merely verging on the sentimental, but in the endless dwelling on Lincoln's funeral and the recurring images of aged veterans, becoming out-and-out mawkish. Throughout the series, Burns focuses on specific personalities—soldiers, statesmen, loved ones on the home front—to humanize the story of the war and bring its protagonists to life through their often eloquent letters and speeches. The final episode spends much time tracing what happened after the war to these personalities, who include military figures such as William T. Sherman and Nathan B. Forrest, along with persons like Mary Todd Lincoln and Alexander H. Stephens. But in the absence of any historical framework in which to place these stories, their significance is lost. General Philip Sheridan, we are told, ended up fighting Indians in the West, and Elisha Hunt Rhodes prospered in textile manufacturing. But these and other statements exist as disembodied "facts," divorced from the political, economic, and other contexts that give them meaning.

Given that Burns has little interest in the legacy of emancipation, it is not surprising that of the 28 persons (by my count) whose postwar careers are mentioned only two are black: reunion, apparently, was a concern only to whites. One of these blacks is Frederick Douglass, who, we are told, continued his advocacy of civil rights. The other is Hiram Revels, elected in 1870 from Mississippi as the first black member of the U. S. Senate. Although many would regard him as a figure of some importance, Burns introduces Revels simply as an oddity, a foil to underscore the humiliation of Jefferson Davis and the South, since he took the seat once held by the Confederate president. There is no effort to explain who Revels was, how or why he became the first black American to occupy a seat in either house of Congress, what was the larger significance of his election, or what happened to him after his term in office.

Revels could have provided an interesting point of entry into the Reconstruction era.[3] For the record, he was one of well over one thousand black men who held public office during the decade known to historians as Radical Reconstruction (1867–77). Their advent symbolized the revolution in American life wrought by Union victory in the Civil War and the destruction of slavery. Reconstruction was a time of intense conflict over the implications of the North's triumph, in which former slaves sought to breathe substantive meaning into the freedom they had so recently acquired. In demanding an end to the myriad injustices of slavery, incorporation as equal citizens into the political order, autonomy in their personal and religious lives, access to education, and land of their own, African Americans helped to establish the agenda of this dramatic period.

In 1865 and 1866, Lincoln's successor Andrew Johnson became locked in a bitter dispute with Congress. Johnson's policy of giving the white South a free hand in shaping the region's future was challenged by a Republican Congress that rewrote federal law and the Constitution to guarantee their own vision of the war's legacy. In civil rights legislation and in the Thirteenth, Fourteenth, and Fifteenth Amendments, Congress announced its commitment to equality before the law, regardless of race, as the definition of American citizenship, and declared the national state to be the protector of the fundamental rights of all Americans. Although primarily conceived for the purpose of protecting and enfranchising blacks, these measures are not simply a concern of African-American history; rather, they are essential to an understanding of the war's legacy. Transcending boundaries of race and region, they redefined freedom for all Americans.

The decision in 1867 to award black men in the South the right to vote repudiated the prewar tradition that America was a "white man's government" and inaugurated the nation's first experiment in interracial democracy. Even if the new governments that came to power throughout the South were sometimes marred by corruption, they implemented numerous changes in southern life that were forward looking and progressive—establishing the region's first public school systems, attempting to rebuild its shattered economy, passing laws to guarantee the equal civil and political rights of black Americans. These policies inspired a wave of opposition from the majority of white southerners, some of whom formed terrorist organizations like the Ku Klux Klan, which attacked and murdered supporters of Reconstruction in order to drive the new governments from office. In the 1870s, as the northern commitment to Reconstruction and the ideal of racial equality waned, Democrats regained control of one southern state after another. By 1877, Reconstruction had come to an end and white supremacy had been restored throughout the old Confederacy. But in modern debates over the implementation of civil rights laws, the interpretation of the Fourteenth Amendment, and the nation's responsibility to ensure equal opportunity for all its citizens, Reconstruction remains a touchstone and, hence, a continuing force in our lives.

To this turbulent period and the issues it raises Burns devotes exactly two minutes. The word "Reconstruction" is never mentioned, and what little information there is about the era is random and misleading. We are told, for instance, that the former slaves received "nothing but freedom," but no attempt is made to explain what the freed people understood by freedom, why the nation did not grant that to them, or what elements of freedom they did, in fact, acquire. Promises to the former slaves, intones the narrator, were "overlooked in the scramble for a new prosperity," a partial and ultimately meaningless summary of a bitter history of commitment and betrayal. Of Grant's presidency, we learn only that it was corrupt; unmentioned is his willingness to use the power of the federal government to suppress the Ku Klux Klan's heinous acts of violence against southern Republicans. The Klan itself is alluded to only as part of the postwar career of General Nathan B. Forrest, the organization's most prominent founder who, it is said, quit the Klan when it became "too violent." Accompanying this bizarre comment (which seems to imply that some violence against the former slaves was perfectly acceptable) is an image of Klansmen in full regalia marching through the streets of Washington a half-century later. The visual impression is of that of a social club, although clothed in white robes, not a band of violent criminals.

Even when accurate, the "facts" about Reconstruction have next to no historical meaning because they exist outside any historical context. We are told, for instance, that Mississippi spent fully one-fifth of its 1865 budget on artificial limbs for former soldiers. But the significance of this "fact" is rather more complicated than Burns seems to appreciate. Mississippi's government was elected by and for whites, and the limbs were for Confederate veterans alone, their purchase authorized by the same legislature that enacted the infamous Black Code that sought to reduce the former slaves to a status reminiscent of slavery. In fact, more men from Mississippi fought in the Union army than the Confederate army, but the tens of thousands of black veterans from the state, like all African Americans, simply did not form part of the community served by the new government. Had Mississippi provided artificial limbs for *all* veterans who needed them, the cost would have been higher still. On the other hand, since Mississippi's planters were essentially unwilling to tax themselves (a large proportion of state revenue came from "head" taxes on individuals, regardless of income, rather than on the value of land), the state budget was extremely low, making the figure of one-fifth perhaps less impressive than appears at first glance. Had the Mississippi legislature taken seriously its responsibilities, had it raised money, say, to provide public education for the state's children, the percentage of the budget allocated to artificial limbs would have been substantially less. My point is not that Burns should have explored all these issues in depth; simply that this particular item of expenditure, offered as a sentimental reminder of the war's human cost, might as easily have been used to illustrate the quality of postwar "reconciliation" and the ways the white southerners returned to power by Andrew Johnson defined the parameters of black freedom and the social responsibilities of government. This, however, would have required the filmmaker to take an interest in the struggle in postwar America to define the consequences of emancipation.

The decision to ignore Reconstruction is especially unfortunate because treating the era in greater depth would have given meaning to Barbara Fields's remark that the Civil War has not yet ended. The postwar story of Reconstruction and its overthrow, of the making and waning of a national commitment to equality, drives the point home by suggesting the historical origins of modern racial problems, thus connecting the past with the present. Instead, as so often in the series, Fields's trenchant remark becomes not the inspiration for an investigation of history, but a substitute for it. Her comment is treated as a "sound bite" and, as is so often the case, its impact is undercut by the visual images that accompany it—in this case newsreels of the 1913 and 1938 Gettysburg reunions. Faced with a choice between historical illumination or nostalgia, Burns consistently opts for nostalgia.

Like Alexandra Ripley, whose novel *Scarlett* has the heroine of *Gone With the Wind* implausibly wait out the Reconstruction era in Ireland, Burns chooses to ignore the contentious history of post-Civil War America. One cannot ascribe this omission to the absence of compelling visual images and first-person testimonies of the sort used elsewhere in the series. The same libraries and archives that contain the thousands of Civil War photographs Burns utilized to such telling effect in earlier episodes also possess dramatic photographs and engravings of former slaves, Klansmen, and scenes on postwar plantations. The poignancy of the letters and diaries that gave such immediacy to other parts of the series are equaled or exceeded by the moving letters, petitions, and statements before Congressional committees by freedpeople and white southerners responding to the profound changes wrought by the Civil War. It is a failure of historical imagination, not the absence of historical material suitable for television, that explains the structure and subject matter of the final episode.

Let me make myself perfectly clear. The issue here is not, primarily, one of "coverage" but of interpretation. Ignoring the actual history of postwar America (which necessarily distorts understanding of the war itself) arises inevitably from a vision of the Civil War as a family quarrel among whites, whose fundamental accomplishment was the preservation of the Union and in which the destruction of slavery was a side issue and African Americans little more than a problem confronting white society. Even on its own terms, however, the treatment of "reunion" is wholly inadequate, for Burns does not appear to realize that the process involved far more than simply reknitting the shattered bonds of nationhood.

A nation is not merely a form of government, a material entity, or a distinct people, but, in Benedict Anderson's celebrated phrase, an "imagined community."[4] Its boundaries are internal as well as external, intellectual as well as geographic. And the process of "imagining" is itself contentious and ultimately political. Who constructs the community, who has the power to enforce a certain definition of nationality, will determine where the boundaries of inclusion and exclusion lie, who stands within or outside them. If the Civil War created the modern American nation, the specific character that reunion took helped to define what kind of nation America was to be. Reunion represented a substantial retreat from the Reconstruction ideal of a color-blind citizenship. The road to reunion was paved with the broken dreams of black Americans, and the betrayal of those dreams was indispensable to the process of reunion as it actually took place. This was why Frederick Douglass fought in the 1870s and 1880s not only for civil rights, as the final episode mentions, but to remind Americans of the war's causes and meaning. Douglass dreaded the implications of reunion, if it simply amounted to "peace among the whites."[5] Yet Burns seems unable to understand reunion in any other way.

Reunion took place not in a vacuum but in a specific historical context, marked by the rise of a xenophobic patriotism "imagining" the reunited nation via the language of racial exclusiveness. By ignoring this context (which included the disenfranchisement and segregation of blacks in the South, the exclusion by federal statute of Chinese immigrants, and the emergence of the United States as an overseas imperial power in the Spanish-American War), Burns surrenders the possibility of probing the costs of reunion as well as its benefits. Is it not worthy of note that 1913 witnessed not only the Gettysburg commemoration, but Woodrow Wilson's order segregating federal offices in Washington, D.C.? In treating reconciliation as a straightforward, unproblematic historical process, Burns misses a golden opportunity to explore the ways the process of reunion was linked to a specific definition of the national purpose and character, and a particular understanding of the meaning of the Civil War.

For years, historians have been aware that historical memory is unavoidably selective and historical traditions "invented" and manipulated. Forgetting some aspects of the past is as much a part of historical understanding as remembering others. Selective readings of the past, often institutionalized in rituals like veterans' reunions and publically constructed monuments, help give citizens a shared sense of national identity. In the case of the Civil War, reunion was predicated on a particular interpretation of the conflict's causes and legacy. On the road to reunion, the war was "remembered" not as the crisis of a nation divided by antagonistic labor systems and political and social ideologies, but as a tragic conflict within the American family, whose great bloodshed was in many ways meaningless, but which accomplished the essential task of solidifying a united nation. Its purpose, in other words, was preservation, not transformation. Both sides, in this view, were composed of brave men fighting for noble principles (Union in the case of the North, self-determination on the part of the South)—a vision exemplified by the late nineteenth-century cults of Lincoln and Lee, each representing the noblest features of his society and each a figure on whom Americans of all regions could look back with pride. In this story, the war's legacy lay essentially in the soldiers themselves, their valor and ultimate reconciliation, not in any ideological causes or purposes. The struggle against slavery was a minor feature of the war, and the abolition of slavery worthy of note essentially for removing a cause of dissension among white Americans.[6]

This view of the war was popularized at the very veterans' reunions on which Burns dwells so extensively, where black veterans were nearly invisible (as they are in the final episode). It was reflected in the hundreds of Civil War monuments which, with only two or three exceptions, failed to include a single representation of a black soldier. It was given scholarly expression in the work of turn-of-the-century "nationalist" historians like James Ford Rhodes and Edward B. McMaster, and popularized for a mass audience in D. W. Griffith's *The Birth of a Nation*, a cinematic paean to national unity and white supremacy that received its premiere at Woodrow Wilson's White House. A particular understanding of Reconstruction, "remembered" by Griffith as a misguided attempt to raise African Americans to a status of political and civil equality for which they were congenitally incompetent, played a central role in this story. For Griffith, as for his generation, black suffrage was the gravest error of the entire Civil War period. Frank acknowledgment of the "failure" of Reconstruction and the incapacity of black Americans provided one foundation of the nation "born" after the Civil War, a point on which white Americans, North and South, could agree as part of the process of reunion. It was the complicity of academic historians in legitimating this interpretation of the war and Reconstruction that led W. E. B. DuBois to offer an irrefutable indictment of the historical profession in "The Propaganda of History," the final chapter of his great work *Black Reconstruction in America.*[7]

This interpretation survived for decades because it accorded with deeply entrenched American political and social realities—the abrogation, with northern acquiescence, of the Fourteenth and Fifteenth Amendments in the South, the elimination of the Republican party from southern politics, the widespread conviction that southern whites knew better than northern meddlers how to deal with their region's "race problem." Decades ago, historians abandoned this view of the Civil War era; today most view slavery as the war's fundamental cause, emancipation as central to its meaning and consequences, and Reconstruction as a praiseworthy if flawed effort to establish the principle of equal rights for all Americans. Yet throughout the Burns series, there are disturbing echoes of this older interpretation of the war and Reconstruction. Emancipation is essentially presented as a gift by Lincoln to blacks, the role of black soldiers is given scant attention, and Reconstruction, as we have seen, all but ignored. (In the 500-page book accompanying the television series, Reconstruction is referred to a total of three times, one of which is Shelby Foote's characterization of the period as "really cruel," a reiteration of the traditional view that granting equal rights to blacks should primarily be understood as a punishment for southern whites.)[8]

The final episode presents the veterans' reunions as moments of "brotherly love and affection," embodiments of the fact that northerners and southerners (at least white ones) had come to recognize their common heroism and humanity. As former Congressman James Symington comments, both sides "shared a common love of liberty" even though (in a homey but incoherent metaphor) they gave it "different English as it spun through their lives." In a speech during the war, Abraham Lincoln offered the best answer to this kind of sophistry:[9]

> We all declare for liberty; but in using the same *word* we do not all mean the same *thing*. With some the word liberty may mean for each man to do as he pleases with himself, and the product of his labor; while with others the same word may mean for some men to do as they please with other men, and the product of other men's labor. Here are two, not only different, but incompatible things, called by the same name—liberty . . . [Today] we behold the processes by which thousands are daily passing from under the yoke of bondage, hailed by some as the advance of liberty, and bewailed by others as the destruction of all liberty.

Neither Symington nor the narrator quite gets around to appreciating Lincoln's point that the southern definition of liberty rested on the power to enslave others, for this would suggest that the South fought for slavery as much as for freedom.

All in all, ignoring Reconstruction or casting it as an unfortunate era of corruption and misgovernment, and expelling blacks from the account of the war's aftermath, are not so much oversights, but an exercise in selective remembering not unlike that practiced by white Americans of the post-Civil War generation. Rather than subjecting it to critical analysis, Burns recapitulates the very historical understanding of the war "invented" in the 1890s as part of the glorification of the national state and the nationwide triumph of white supremacy. The final episode is not so much an account of how and why a particular understanding of the meaning of the Civil War flourished in post-Reconstruction America but an embodiment and reinforcement of that very understanding.

Americans have always had an ambivalent relationship with history. "We have it in our power to begin the world over again," Thomas Paine announced in 1776 in arguing for American independence: the past was, quite simply, irrelevant. Unlike many other nations, it is, in a sense, our putative destiny rather than a long-established history that orders our sense of ourselves as a community. Since the Civil War, that sense of national purpose has been intimately tied up with a selective memory of the conflict and what came after it. Accurately remembered, the events of Reconstruction place the issue of racial justice on the agenda of modern American life. But not if the history of that era and the costs paid on the road to reunion are ignored, misrepresented, or wished away.

7

Telling the Story:
The Historian, the Filmmaker,
and the Civil War

LEON F. LITWACK

WHAT D.W. GRIFFITH'S *The Birth of a Nation* did for the history of American cinema and popular perceptions of Reconstruction, Ken Burns's *The Civil War* did three-quarters of a century later for documentary television and popular perceptions of the most epic theme in American history. Both employed technology creatively and imaginatively. Both enjoyed immense popularity. Both demonstrated the extraordinary power of film to convey images, to portray historical events, and to provide Americans with easy explanations of terrible complexities in their history.

Far more persuasively, much more compellingly than any historical work, *The Birth of a Nation* explained Reconstruction and the "Negro problem" to generations of Americans. After viewing the film, one observer could barely restrain himself. This was more than a gripping and epic motion picture.

This was history. "Chicago went wild about the film," he wrote. "It started people to thinking. The people of Chicago saw more in *The Birth of a Nation* than a tremendous dramatic spectacle. They saw in it the reason the South wants to keep the Negro in his place. They saw in it a new conception of Southern problems." It was the first motion picture to be shown in the White House, and President Woodrow Wilson was reported to have said "it is like writing history in lightning. My only regret is that it is all so terribly true." His own popular multi-volume *History of the American People* (published in 1902 and greeted warmly by scholars) was cited in the film as academic support for its historical accuracy.

Over the past century, the power of historians and filmmakers to influence the public, to reflect and shape attitudes and popular prejudices, has been amply demonstrated, often with tragic consequences. Rummaging through the past, filmmakers did not simply reinforce prevailing racial, ethnic, and patriotic biases; they helped to create and perpetuate them. The motion picture fixed in the minds of millions of Americans the image of black men and women as a race of buffoons and half-wits, sometimes amusing, sometimes threatening, almost always less than human. Historians, for their part, succeeded in miseducating several generations of Americans. What dominated their perceptions (and distortions) of the past were the views of exceptional people who left the most easily accessible records, the kind of people who possessed the income, leisure, and literacy that permitted them to record their thoughts in journals, diaries, autobiographies, and letters. Historian Richard Hofstadter once wrote of Thomas Jefferson, "The leisure that made possible his great writings on human liberty was supported by the labors of three generations of slaves." The history of working-class men and women, rural and urban, white and black, was thought to be impossible to retrieve because historians relied upon and felt most comfortable with the kinds of records and documents ordinary people have not usually kept.

The way history is interpreted, taught, and portrayed on the screen does have consequences. African Americans, in particular, have seen the cinema and historical scholarship used frequently and effectively to reinforce and perpetuate racial stereotypes that underscored their inferiority and justified their repression. For years, filmmakers provided audiences a view of slavery that acted out the version propagated in one of the leading textbooks of American history, co-authored by two eminent historians, Samuel Eliot Morison of Harvard University and Henry Steele Commager of Columbia University. "As for Sambo," they insisted, "there is some reason to believe that he suffered less than any other class in the South from its 'peculiar institution.' The majority of slaves were adequately fed, well cared for, and apparently happy. . . . Although brought to America by force, the incurably optimistic Negro soon became attached to the country, and devoted to his 'white folks.'"

The way in which Reconstruction—that unique and complex period of bi-racial democratic government in the South—came to be written, screened, and believed would exert and retain an even more powerful hold on Americans, helping to shape and reinforce white southern (and northern) responses to any challenge to racial segregation or to any proposal to readmit blacks as voters. The dehumanizing images and stereotypes conveyed in textbooks and in films such as *The Birth of a Nation* (the depraved black politician, the grinning

Sambo, and the black rapist) would be deeply imprinted on the white mind, and they continue to resonate to this day.

Over the past three decades, however, the writing and teaching of American history experienced profound, far-reaching changes. The sheer diversity of historical focus opened up new ways of conceptualizing the past and reflected a far greater sensitivity to the complexities and varieties of cultural documentation. Historians came to understand that most men and women, although spending their lives in relative obscurity and never sharing the fruits of affluence or enjoying power, nevertheless have found ways to relate their experiences and to communicate their feelings about matters of daily and far-reaching concern to them.

Working-class people have never been inarticulate. The neglect of their lives by historians revealed not so much an absence of sources as a failure of historical imagination and commitment. But that neglect has been redressed in recent decades, as historians learned to appreciate enormous possibilities they had seldom considered: the value of music, art, dance, humor, folklore, oral remembrances, photography, and film as cultural records and interpretive documents, the various ways in which these sources illuminate, often with a frightening honesty, the range and depth of the human experience and document the innermost thoughts and preoccupations of Americans. "How much history can be transmitted by pressure on a guitar string?" Robert Palmer asks in *Deep Blues*. "The thought of generations," he answers, "the history of every human being who's ever felt the blues come down like showers of rain."

By expanding the range of cultural documentation, historians were able to bring to historical consciousness people ordinarily left outside the framework of the American experience. The new sources gave voice to previously marginalized men and women and transformed profoundly how we define this nation. What has always seemed to most Americans distinctive about their heritage is freedom. That is what sets the United States off from much of the world, and to listen to most Presidents, that explains the uniqueness of this nation. But that is to read American history without the presence of African Americans, to define them out of American identity, to exclude a people who enjoyed neither liberty, nor impartial government, nor the equal protection of the law. Once you incorporate the African American into American history, as historian Nathan Huggins pointedly observed, you might be forced to reinterpret the American experience in such a way that *freedom* is not the word that defines it. You might have to change the terms in which you think and talk about American history and American life.

The recent work of historians has, in fact, altered the ways in which we think, talk, and write about the past. American history will never be the same again. Voices and dialogues long stifled, the experiences of peoples once marginalized or ignored are now being heard and integrated into the study of history. Filmmakers, however, have not kept pace with these changes. With some important exceptions (Julie Dash's *Daughters of the Dust*, for example), they have yet to incorporate into their work many of the new voices, perspectives, and cultural experiences. The history portrayed on the screen, both in Hollywood and documentary films, all too often betrays an ignorance of or indifference to recent historical advances. Filmmakers may be innovative in the techniques they employ but the history imparted is by and large traditional, conventional history. And it is usually safe, risk-free, inoffensive, upbeat, reassuring, comforting, optimistic history, more often than not an exercise in self-congratulation and a celebration of consensus.

The Civil War is a notable example. Its popular success was not altogether unmerited. Skillfully crafted, technically innovative, evocative and emotionally seductive, the television series made effective use of letters, diaries and journals, archival photographs, paintings, broadsides, newsreel footage, eyewitness accounts, and an often mesmerizing musical score. Nine episodes in eleven hours afforded the producers and writers an extraordinary, unprecedented opportunity to explore in some depth the wide range of experiences making up this conflict, using the new voices and experiences that have so profoundly altered our understanding of the era. Unfortunately, the opportunity was only partially grasped.

The history depicted in *The Civil War*, as distinct from the techniques employed to convey it, is conventional and sometimes suspect. This is largely a story of military struggles, featuring the politics of command, the landscape of combat, the tales of courage and devotion, the exploits of Johnny Reb and Billy Yank, the statesmanship of Abraham Lincoln, the nobility of Robert E. Lee, and the essential passivity of blacks and women. And it revives the pernicious notion that once dominated historiography: the war need not have happened at all, if only calmer, more responsible, less radical and extreme heads had prevailed.

To the film's credit, the agony of the Civil War has seldom been more graphically depicted. This is a military history unlike most, in that it strips the war of much of its romance and pageantry. For years, the war's chroniclers chose to dwell on the military tactics, the smell of cannon fire, the picturesque charges. *The Civil War*, on the other hand, examines, relentlessly and often hauntingly, the aftermaths: the exhaustion, the squalor, the shrieks and groans of the wounded, the stacked limbs of the amputees, the bloated corpses, the stench of death and the dying.

The cost in human life was enormous, and viewers are never permitted to lose sight of that enormity. Some 3 million Americans fought in the war, and more than 623,000 Americans died (in a nation of 31.5 million), exceeding all of this nation's wars combined, including Vietnam. Nearly as many Americans were wounded and permanently debilitated. *The Civil War* reminds us, too, that at Shiloh in two days more Americans died than in all previous American wars, that at Cold Harbor some 7000 Americans fell in 20 minutes, and that in 12 hours of combat along the picturesque banks of a creek called Antietam some 23,000 perished—the bloodiest single day in America's military history, with nothing achieved but a stalemate.

Like the battlefields that continue to attract hundreds of thousands of visitors every year, *The Civil War* is mostly about how men died and how they responded to the call to battle, not why they fought and died. Like the preserved battlefields (dubbed by some Civil War buffs as "sacred ground"), the valor on both sides is commemorated. What the Rebels— badly misnamed—thought they were fighting for is left unclear. Shelby Foote (quoting the Confederate soldier who told a Yankee, "we're fighting because you're down here") suggests that they fought in defense of their homes. Without slavery, however, there would have been no war, no slaughter, and no need to defend their homes. From the very outset, as

Foote (among others) is unwilling to concede, the enslavement of black men and women defined the Confederacy as a nation. Jefferson Davis resented any suggestion that secession had been revolutionary; on the contrary, he and his followers had left the Union "to save ourselves from a revolution." The secession conventions that chose to proclaim the reasons for their action invariably assigned the highest priority to the defense of slavery. Robert E. Lee said during the war that the Confederacy fought to save slavery from destruction. He refused to exchange black prisoners-of-war (since most of them he deemed property), he appeared to have no problem with his troops capturing blacks in Pennsylvania and sending them South into slavery, and as late as 1865 he preferred to think of the enslavement of black men and women not as an evil but "as the best [relation] that can exist between the white and black races."

Alexander H. Stephens, Vice President of the Confederacy, called slavery "the cornerstone" of the Confederate States of America: "its foundations are laid, its cornerstone rests upon the great truth that the negro is not equal to the white man, that slavery—subordination to the superior race—is his natural and normal condition. This, our new government, is the first in the history of the world based upon this great physical, philosophical and moral truth." The white South, slaveholders and nonslaveholders alike, echoed Stephens's words. A North Carolina private wrote a friend in 1863, "You know I am a poor man having none of the property said to be the cause of the present war. But I have a wife and some children to rase [*sic*] in honor and never to be put on an equality with the African race."

Few understood all of this more deeply than the enslaved. The first episode, in fact, briefly suggested *The Civil War* would transcend the military conflict and probe with equal intensity, sensitivity, and resourcefulness how the war came home to families, black and white, in the South. That promise, unfortunately, was not kept. Two major war fronts co-existed during the Civil War: the clash of armies on the battlefields and the social convulsions at home. *The Civil War* stays mostly on the battlefield, virtually ignoring the other war, the conflict fought out on farms and plantations, in towns and cities throughout the South, even where no Union or Confederate soldiers appeared.

This missed opportunity deprived *The Civil War* of an extraordinary moment in American history. None of the "great battles," not even Antietam, Shiloh, or Gettysburg, compare in sheer drama with the way in which the Civil War came to be transformed into a social revolution of such far-reaching proportions and consequences. The white South went to war to achieve independence and to preserve and reinforce the enslavement of its principal labor force—black men and women. But the South's quest for independence would quickly underscore its dependency on black labor and black loyalty and set in motion a social upheaval that proved impossible to contain. In *The Civil War*, despite the abundance of images and resources at the command of the filmmakers, that social upheaval is never played out with the same depth, the same sensitivity, the same emotional and dramatic intensity as the military engagements.

From the moment the Civil War broke out, the nearly four million black men and women of the South were placed in an anomalous and dangerous position—in an impossible position. They were the muscle of a military and economic effort designed to perpetuate their enslavement. On the one hand, they were the cause of the war; on the other, they were necessary for the war's success—that is, their labor and loyalty were essential to the Confederacy. But with their freedom at stake, could they be trusted? The answer came slowly in some cases, quickly in others: the more desperate the Confederate cause, the more the white South depended on the labor and loyalty of black men and women. And the more they were needed, the closer they came to freedom and the less they could be trusted.

Neither whites nor blacks were untouched by the physical and emotional demands of the war. Both races suffered, and each evinced some sympathy for the plight of the other. But there was a critical difference, and that difference grew in importance with each passing month. If slaves evinced a compassion for beleaguered masters and mistresses, if they deplored the ruin of the land and crops by Union soldiers who brutalized and looted whites and blacks alike, many of these same slaves and still others came to appreciate at some moment in the war that in the very suffering and defeat of their "white folks" lay their only hope for freedom.

No wonder, then, the Civil War conveyed such conflicting historical memories in the South. For white southerners, the Confederacy, the stars and bars, and Johnny Reb would assume legendary proportions. But for black southerners, the ultimate significance of the Confederacy lay in its destruction. What for generations of whites remained a heroic struggle for independence took on a very different meaning for black southerners. To have prolonged the life of the Confederacy was to prolong their own enslavement and debasement. That revelation was no less far-reaching in its implications than the acknowledgment by growing numbers of white southerners that they were facing danger on two fronts: from the Yankees and from their own blacks.

The experience of the Civil War is replete with tragedy and contradiction, complexity and enigma, ambiguity and irony. It is the remarkable story of how enslaved black men and women, as much as any act of Congress or presidential proclamation, helped to free themselves and undermine the authority of the planter class. What the Civil War did was to sweep away the pretenses, dissolve the illusions, and lay bare the tensions and instability inherent in the master-slave relationship. For many white families who owned slaves, it was a terrible moment of truth. The war taught the owner who claimed to "know" his Negroes best that he knew them least of all, that he had mistaken their docility for contentment, their deference and accommodation for submission. Few white families knew their blacks well enough to be able to determine when a longtime faithful might suddenly reach the breaking point and no longer feel obliged to tolerate the arrogance of the white families for whom she worked. Many years later, white southerners preferred to ignore this "moment of truth," opting for stories of black duty and loyalty. The selectivity with which whites chose to recall the wartime behavior of blacks is understandable; the failure of *The Civil War* to document this dramatic and critical historical moment is less comprehensible.

Neither the North nor the South had anticipated the transformation of the Civil War into a struggle over the meaning of freedom in America. That theme, briefly suggested at the outset, is not sustained with the same documentary depth and vigor as are the military engagements; indeed, there is a certain tension, unstated and perhaps unintended, between commentators Barbara Fields and Shelby Foote over the relative importance of the military struggle and the internal social convulsions. If measured by film footage, Foote is the over-whelming victor. Used all too sparingly, Fields and various black voices try to bring us back to first principles, to what the violence and dying were all about.

What *The Civil War* needed to explore were the ways in which the conflict revolutionized black expectations. In that brief flurry of excitement and anticipation at the moment of freedom—in the fields, the kitchens, the quarters—there was bold talk of new ways of living and working, and being able to do what the white folks did. This was a moment of intense hope for black southerners, a moment of terrifying promise, when they glimpsed other possibilities in their lives. The documentation of this moment is readily available, and its importance can hardly be exaggerated. What happened to that spirit, to that determination, to those hopes and expectations would profoundly affect race relations and the nation for the next century.

It is not as though *The Civil War* ignored blacks. On the contrary, black faces and black expression figure more prominently than in most cinematic treatments of the war. Slavery is examined with some depth in the first episode, and blacks appear in a number of capacities. But the treatment, as in the episode "The Breath of Emancipation," is insufficient to convey the diverse ways in which enslaved black men and women helped to disrupt the labor system and undermine the Confederacy. The treatment of emancipation perpetuates the traditional but erroneous and simplistic view of President Lincoln as the Great Emancipator, single-handedly breaking the shackles of bondage. The brief section on the belated decision to recruit black troops into the Confederate Army never speaks to the reaction of black southerners. ("They asked me if I would fight for my country," a Virginia black recalled. "I said, 'I have no country.'") And although the film treats blacks in the Union Army, it fails to comprehend their significance. It is no more successful than *Glory* in capturing the extraordinary transformation by which uniformed and armed black men, most of them recently slaves, marched through the southern countryside as an army of occupation and liberation. For many whites, no moment in the entire war brought more anguish, fear, and humiliation. Although visually depicted, black soldiers are assigned little more of a role in *The Civil War* than in Shelby Foote's three-volume history: "Negro troops proved that they could stop bullets and shells as well as white men, but that was about all." That was not "all," as both white and black observers readily agreed, if for different reasons.

In much that is written and filmed about the South, the perverse assumption persists that southerners are necessarily white. When Shelby Foote uses the term "southerners," he is invariably talking about white southerners, though he never tells us that. To say, for example, as Foote does, that southerners saw in the election of Lincoln a threat to their institutions is to distort the historical record. Many black southerners saw in the election of Lincoln, as in the advance of the Union Army and each Confederate defeat, the promise of freedom. If "southerners" is defined to include blacks as well as whites, it becomes highly debatable how many southerners actually supported the Confederacy. One might suggest, for example, that nearly as many Mississippians opposed as fought to defend the Confederacy—if one dispels the myth of white unity and counts the substantial number of black men (and some whites) who enlisted in the Union Army, the many more blacks who in various ways undermined the war effort and welcomed their liberation, and the depletion of the Confederate forces by desertions and absenteeism.

Perhaps no film, not even an eleven-hour production, can cover adequately each of the massive themes that make up the Civil War and its aftermath. But in *The Civil War* the meaning and legacy of this bloody conflict, including the dramatic social revolution it helped to unleash, simply becomes lost in the detailed accounts of combat and command. Like so many historians, Ken Burns and his staff permitted themselves to be overwhelmed if not imprisoned by the ready availability of sources that told (albeit often eloquently) only part of the story, omitting a wide range of historical participants. Although *The Civil War* provides viewers with many fleeting glances of ordinary black men and women, they are seldom given any voice. The staff made full use of the abundant documentation of the military struggle. If they had been as resourceful and imaginative in using the southern landscape, including surviving plantation houses and slave quarters, along with the letters of black soldiers, the dispatches of black reporters and chaplains, the remembrances of black observers (women and men) and participants, and the journals and letters of white southerners which provided a detailed, often anguished record of black behavior, *The Civil War* would have been heightened dramatically and far more faithful to the historical record.

The most appalling and revealing shortcoming in Ken Burns's *The Civil War* is the way it chose to deal with the war's legacy—what it said and what it did not say. With the passage of time, Americans came to be increasingly selective in their memories of the war. With every anniversary, with every reunion of aging veterans, the war came to be depoliticized;

the more compelling (and controversial) moral issues were pushed further into the background. Memories on both sides turned toward a recounting of military exploits, toward patriotic sentimentalism. What causes (if any) might have impelled some 623,000 young Americans to lay down their lives became increasingly irrelevant. What mattered was not what they had died for but how they had died. By the late nineteenth century, one would hardly have known that slavery had anything to do with the war or that blacks had participated in any way except as passive recipients of their freedom or as loyal and submissive servants.

The reunions of veterans, as depicted in *The Civil War* in old photographs and newsreel footage, provided the perfect opportunity to examine the war's legacy and how the survivors ultimately came to grips with its underlying issues and enduring tensions. By the 1890s, the heroic artifacts and statuary of the Lost Cause had proliferated almost in proportion to southern whites retaking the ground they had lost in the war. Once the wartime wounds had healed, the Lost Cause monopolized the popular literature and ultimately won over the hearts and minds of the victors. "The South surrendered at Appomattox," Albion W. Tourgee declared, but "the North has been surrendering ever since." Thirty-two years after the war, in 1897, President McKinley told a convention of Civil War veterans, "The army of Grant and the army of Lee are one now in faith, in hope, in fraternity, in purpose, and in an invincible patriotism."

The nation had been reborn, and it is this rebirth that Ken Burns chooses to celebrate in *The Civil War*. The last episode invokes the nostalgic reunions of the Blue and the Gray to underscore and celebrate national reunification and the birth of the modern American nation, while ignoring the brutality, violence, and racial repression on which that reconciliation rested. Even as the aging veterans greeted each other, shook hands, and embraced in "brotherly love and affection," suggesting that this had been a needless war, whites were using their political experience and military superiority, their ownership of the land, control of credit, vagrancy laws, blacklists, the courts, and the police, along with the mystique of the "lost cause," to reimpose their will. What the white South lost on the battlefield it would ultimately win back through legal repression (disfranchisement, segregation, and peonage), ritualized public murders, terrorism, and intimidation. (*The Birth of a Nation* also celebrated the reunification of white America but chose at the same time to celebrate and justify the terrorism that made it possible.)

When Americans commemorated the centennial of the Civil War between 1961 and 1965, the glamour and nostalgia blurred almost entirely the issues that had precipitated the war. The most memorable moments of the Centennial were unscheduled and coincidental: the civil rights demonstrations in which mostly young black southerners insisted upon completing the tasks left undone by the Civil War. On a new set of battlefields, in places like Montgomery, Selma, Birmingham, Jackson, Little Rock, Boston, Chicago, and Los Angeles, still another struggle would be waged over the meaning of freedom in America.

It is left to Ulysses S. Grant, the military victor, to utter perhaps the most poignant observation about the American Civil War in these eleven hours. He has come to Appomattox Court House to accept the surrender of Lee's Army of Northern Virginia. He finds himself "sad and depressed" by this meeting with his vanquished foe. Lee and his men had fought so long and so valiantly; they had suffered such immense losses for their cause. But for what purpose? The cause which led them to the battlefield and for which so many of them died, Grant reflected, "was, I believe, one of the worst for which people ever fought." No amount of historical revisionism, no amount of sentimentalism about Johnny Reb fighting for his home and family can erase that fundamental truth about the American Civil War.

This was not, as Bruce Catton once argued, "the needless war" which might have been settled by "reasonable men of good will." Nor is Shelby Foote persuasive when he suggests (perfectly consistent with the film's spirit) that the war came "because we failed to do the thing we really have a genius for, which is compromise." He says nothing about what might have been compromised, but those who lived at the time, especially blacks, knew very well what would have been the basis for any new sectional compromise. Shelby Foote is an engaging battlefield guide, a master of the anecdote, and a gifted and charming story teller, but he is not a good historian. He seems to have little idea as to what gave meaning to this "enormous catastrophe" other than the valor of the combatants. Barbara Fields argued that the struggle for black freedom made it a very different kind of war, that the slavery issue ennobled the war, turning the otherwise meaningless carnage into something higher and nobler. But Foote is unable to grasp this critical point and he will have none of it. When asked in an interview to respond to Fields's observation, Foote vigorously dissented. "I don't think it ennobled the war; I think it dirtied up the war." And, he insisted, "Black contribution to the war was overemphasized"—a perfectly explicable statement from a person who has demonstrated no knowledge or understanding of that contribution.

The inescapable tragedy of the Civil War is that it had to be fought. The cause of human freedom required no less. If the Union had been preserved without abolishing slavery, it would not have been a Union worth saving. If the South had made good on its quest for independence, it would have perpetuated the enslavement of black men and women. The white South lost the war, not the black South. The white South, however, won the peace, and we continue to live with the consequences. For the four million freed slaves, as the final episode briefly suggests, the content of their newly won freedom remained unresolved. It is Barbara Fields who makes this critical point, adding that the Civil War is in many ways still being fought and may still be lost. By this time, however, her voice carries little weight, and Shelby Foote is again permitted the last word. "The truth is," he insists, "that if we'd been anything like as superior as we think we are, we would never have fought that war." That is more consistent with the theme and spirit this film conveys, though Burns opted for a more upbeat conclusion. In the end, Barbara Fields's vision of a Civil War that is still being fought and may yet be lost and Ken Burns's romantic vision of the war's legacy are simply irreconcilable.

Drawing on the "new history," filmmakers and historians can strike a productive collaboration in documenting the many different ways in which men and women have experienced the United States. Filmmakers have the opportunity to introduce people, dialogues, and experiences long repressed by restrictive and unimaginative historical scholarship and cinematography. Historians of the American people, if they hope to reach more than a handful of those people, need to write history that is readable and that does not sacrifice the dramatic narrative to a rapidly proliferating analytic jargon. Both filmmakers and historians need to engage the public in the social complexity and diversity of the past, and to do so in ways that are conceptually persuasive, using a variety of individuals, events, ideas, and cultural documents. They need to bring into historical consciousness the perceptions and experiences of people—women and men—ordinarily left outside the framework of history, many of them losers in their own time, outlaws, rebels who—individually or collectively—tried to flesh out, tried to give meaning to abstract notions of liberty, equality, and freedom, some of whom chose to dissent from the national consensus and opted for the highest kind of patriotism and loyalty to their country—a willingness to unmask its leaders and subject its institutions and ideology to critical examination.

Whether writing history or making historical films, the object is not to replace old lies with new myths, or old omissions and distortions with a new set of heroics and romanticisms. A film about the Civil War, or any other historical subject, should not simply reinforce what Americans already know of their past. Historian Natalie Davis, in speaking of her role in creating *The Return of Martin Guerre*, captured the spirit that should enable historians and filmmakers to work together more effectively, without sacrificing either historical accuracy or dramatic content: "I wanted to shake people up, because I feel that is what history is about. It is not about confirming what you already know, but about stretching it and turning it upside down and then reaffirming some values, or putting some into question."

It is not enough for historians and filmmakers to impart the facts. It is incumbent upon them to make people feel those facts, to make them see and feel those facts in ways that may be genuinely disturbing. The best history, the best films explore different versions of reality, they deepen sensibilities, afflict the comfortable, the complacent, and the indifferent, and make a difference in how people conceptualize, think about, feel (and even act upon) the past. The best history, the best films, break away from conventions and take risks—even disturb the peace. Some 130 years after Appomattox, that "peace" needs to be disturbed, as the meaning of freedom in America—the issue over which the Civil War was fought—remains unresolved.

8

Refighting the Civil War

GEOFFREY C. WARD

*A*s THE PRINCIPAL WRITER for *The Civil War* series, I am all too aware that the script contains its share of errors. I imbedded some of them there myself. The most spectacular must be the fact that we managed to get wrong both the date of Lincoln's assassination and his age at the time of his death. Both errors are mine alone: I somehow confused the April date of Lincoln's murder with the death of another President with whom I am better acquainted, Franklin Roosevelt, and we misstated Lincoln's age mostly because of my lamentable arithmetic. And, unbelievably, through repeated screenings for our distinguished advisers and for ourselves, no one involved seems ever to have noticed either error.

For sins of commission like that we deserve chastening.

And there are sins of omission, too, for which I have personal regrets.

I wish, for example, that we'd done more with women and the home front, but we could never find a way to make their appearances seem much more than interruptions in the midst of the complicated, head-long, largely military story we found ourselves trying to tell. We'd like to have done more with politics, too, but even enlightened PBS viewers have a low tolerance for the subtleties of, say, the Wilmot Proviso.

If a film can be said to have had a "conscience," ours was surely provided by the voices of two African Americans—Frederick Douglass, who tells truth to power from the first episode to the last, and Professor Barbara J. Fields, who eloquently reminded the audience again and again of what finally made the war worthwhile, of how vital was the role played by blacks in their own emancipation.

We were so certain of the power of those presences, reinforced by a rich chorus of other black voices—slaves, freedmen, soldiers, many of whose authentic words were culled from Ira Berlin's monumental *Freedom* series—that we were pretty well prepared for the criticism that came from unreconstructed southern viewers, still persuaded that a struggle over states' rights and not slavery had been the cause of it all. The Sons of the Confederacy who picketed some of Ken's appearances in the South may have looked a little foolish—clad in butternut, wearing sabers—but their anger at us at least seemed understandable. They had seen what we had always intended for everyone to see, what was perfectly plain to most viewers, that the filmmakers shared U.S. Grant's opinion of the men whose surrender he accepted at Appomattox: they had fought bravely and suffered much for "a cause . . . [that was] one of the worst for which a people ever fought, and one for which there was the least excuse."

I was therefore personally astonished by the much more vigorous assaults launched upon us by others, mostly members of the academic community, who evidently saw our whole enterprise as little more than an exercise in racism. Professor Leon Litwack has accused us of having sought to perpetuate the myth of the "essential passivity" of black people; Professor Jeannie Addie has suggested elsewhere that we sought to convey the bizarre notion that "a war to end chattel slavery was a wasteful enterprise"; and Professor Eric Foner alleges that since our film on the Civil War did not also detail Reconstruction, "Burns has little interest in the legacy of emancipation." (The recent series *Baseball*, with its consistent emphasis on race, presumably cleared up that misconception.)

It's hard for me to believe these critics were watching the film we made, the one the late Ralph Ellison saw, for example. I was lucky enough to be introduced to him at a New York reception about two years before he died. He was polite as I stumbled through clumsy words of appreciation for all that his extraordinary writings had meant to me. Then, someone told him I'd been involved in making *The Civil War*.

"Thank you," he said, gripping my hand again. "That show helped everybody know what my folks did back then, what they went through."

No review could possibly have meant more.

Professor Litwack accuses us of "celebra[ting] the reconciliation of the North and South while ignoring the brutal and violent repression which that reconciliation represented." But, we did not ignore it. For the record, the script reads as follows:

Four million Americans had been freed after four years of agony, but the full meaning of that freedom remained unresolved. The Thirteenth Amendment was followed by a four-teenth and a fifteenth, which promised full citizenship and due process of the law for all American men, white and black. But those promises were soon overlooked in the scramble for a new prosperity, and white supremacy was bru-tally reimposed throughout the old Confederacy. The white South won that war of attrition, and it would take another century before blacks regained much of the ground for which so many men had given their lives.

It must be remembered that by the time those lines are heard, we are nearing the end of a very long series about the Civil War; we are not at the beginning of one about Recon-struction or its ugly aftermath. Those subjects—no less compelling, no less important for anyone who wants to under-stand who Americans have been and who we still are—await other filmmakers. (By the logic which dictates that a film about the Civil War must also include the full story of Reconstruc-tion, it seems to me, anyone making a film about the First World War, would have to include the Second, anyone trying to cover the Great Society would also have to assess the Reagan Revolution that was in part a response to it.)

I, too, wish we could have done more with the genu-ine revolution that swept through the slaveholding South as freedom came. But I do believe that we did more with that revolution than anyone else had ever done on film, and it was only the special demands of documentary filmmaking that kept us from doing still more. Before anything else, film demands something to look at. Sadly, there are very few pho-tographs that even hint at the turmoil Professor Litwack (and we) wanted portrayed; certainly, I know of none we failed to include.

And, just as sadly, there is precious little written evidence of the sort we would have needed to fill our our script. Despite the pioneering scholarship of Kenneth Stampp, Herbert G. Gutman, Eugene D. Genovese, Ira Berlin, Barbara Fields, Professor Litwack, and others that has brought forth from various archives an astonishing amount of fresh material (upon which we gratefully drew throughout our series), it is by definition fragmentary. To our great regret, nothing we could find provided enough information about any *individual* slaves to sustain the sort of first-person self-portraits over five years of war that we were able to create for many of our white protagonists.

To do the story of emancipation fuller justice would therefore have demanded that we use the very techniques Professor Litwack has applauded us elsewhere for having avoided— staged re-creations with wholly created dialogue. In the right hands, those techniques can be hugely effective, but they would not have worked within a film otherwise composed of authentic materials.

At the risk of sounding over-sensitive, may I add that some of the criticism in this volume seems needlessly shrill: so ordinarily careful a scholar as Professor Litwack, for example, must know that comparing our series with D.W. Griffith's virulently racist *The Birth of a Nation* is both ludicrous and personally offensive. And some of it just seems silly. Surely, it's better that General Schwartzkopf watched our series than, say, *Patton*, while directing the Gulf War; there is precious little glory in the war we portrayed on-screen. *Of course*, rather than float above the battlefields, describing the distant movements of faceless armies, we chose to depict great battles like Fredericksburg and Gettysburg through the eyes of individual characters whose fates have been made to matter to the audience. And it should not be necessary to explain to members of the academic community that by including one historian's opinion among several on matters over which scholars continue to differ does not imply that his or her view is to be taken as gospel.

We made mistakes. We did not succeed at everything we tried. I even wish we could do over some sequences, just as I'd like to rewrite paragraphs in one or another of the books I've written. But more than that I wish, as someone who both writes history and biography and helps make films, that some way can be found for filmmakers and historians to work together in the future with less recrimination.

I have never taught history. But I did put in five years as editor of *American Heritage*, trying to make authentic history as widely accessible as possible on paper. And after that I spent eight happy years off and on, hidden away in various archives, seeking to solve the riddle of Franklin Roosevelt's personality, and therefore I share with professional historians the knowledge that there is nothing like discovering things for the first time, nothing to compare with making one's way along corridors where no one else's footsteps have sounded before.

For me, working on films only rarely rivals that kind of excitement. It is, by nature, a collaborative art—being on a team is never quite as much fun as being one's own master. And there are things film can simply never do as well as the written word can.

Time imposes crippling restraints.

Television is better at narrative than analysis, better at evoking emotions than expounding complex ideas.

It requires simplification—which can easily lapse into *over*-simplification.

One must resist the temptation to lecture the viewer—or must disguise one's lecturing so skillfully that the viewer's thumb, hovering always now over the channel-changer on his or her remote control, does not take that fatal plunge. (Think what it would be like if students in a lecture hall were similarly equipped.)

Having said all that, I still want to persuade as many historians as I can to think of historical documentaries—and documentary-makers—as allies, not enemies, in the struggle we all seem to be losing to remind our citizenry of who we are and where we came from.

Those who make documentaries badly need the help of historians—and I think it's fair to say that historians need filmmakers' help, too. But beyond that, I think those academics willing to try filmmaking will find it fascinating in its own right.

In the first place, there is the sheer size of the potential audience you can reach with real history. Admittedly, *The Civil War* was a freakish event. The subject seems to come around on the wheel every twenty years or so, and we were very lucky to find ourselves on the right channel at the right time. Still, almost forty million Americans sat and watched more than eleven hours of pretty dense historical narrative, and a gratifying number of them proceeded directly to the nearest bookstore to pick up not only our book, but scores of other Civil War titles that had been languishing on the shelves.

Then, too, documentary-making is filled with challenging choices, choices never encountered in writing traditional history. What does one do when there simply are no authentic images of someone or something essential to the tale you're trying to tell? Is it all right, for example, to use the photograph of a corpse that fell on the second day of Gettysburg as that of someone who died on the first day? We thought so—but only if we could think of no other way to help propel our larger story. But is it all right to show a soldier lying dead on the Gettysburg battlefield as if he had fallen at, say, Glorieta Pass? We thought not—and for that reason could do far less than we would have liked to have done with the whole Western Theater of the war. Since Civil War cameramen by and large did not go west, we could not, finally, spend much time there, either.

The role traditionally played by scholars in the filmmaking process is as advisers, gazetted by the National Endowment for the Humanities, or by the filmmakers themselves, to keep them honest.

In my experience, that relationship has too often been pointlessly wary and adversarial. Scholars worry that they will somehow be co-opted or, worse, financially exploited by venal moviemakers. (In fact, it is the rare documentary that turns a profit. Like graduate students, most filmmakers live from grant to grant.)

Historians are entitled to a serious hearing from the filmmakers who request their time—and I can't deny that there are producers who already know what film they're going to make long before they write their first letter to a potential consultant, who are interested primarily in the scholarly cachet a list of consultants' names lends to the final result. But Ken listens to his advisers. So do the dozen or so other producers with whom I've been lucky enough to work, on *The American Experience* series and elsewhere. All of them understand that accuracy must not be sacrificed for storytelling, that new scholarship demands new kinds of narrative.

It they *don't* listen, any historian worth his per diem should walk out.

But I would ask of academic advisers a reciprocal courtesy, and that is that their counsel be offered in the interest of making things possible, not *im*possible; that they act, until proved wrong, from the assumption that the filmmaker really wants to tell his or her story honestly and wants their help in doing so. The shared objective should be to make a film in which both professor and producer can take pride.

"Critical historians are more or less cannibals," Albert Bushnell Hart told his fellow historians more than three-quarters of a century ago. "They live by destroying each other's conclusions." That was too harsh then and is too harsh now. History will always be an endless argument. Revisionists can count only on being revised. Lively intramural debate among historians over the past forty years has greatly enriched our understanding of our past, demolishing ancient myths, dramatically altering our understanding of episodes we once were sure we understood completely, belatedly restoring to something approaching their rightful place groups largely absent from the history most of us were taught in school.

But the tendency toward cannibalism of which Professor Hart complained is still present at too many historians' conclaves—or so it seems to this veteran of too many such rallies.

In any case, it should be checked at the editing-room door.

9

Four O'Clock in the Morning Courage

KEN BURNS

*E*ARLY IN THE CIVIL WAR, far removed from any of the major fighting, a young fugitive slave named Alex Turner made his way north and eventually joined the 1st New Jersey Cavalry. In the spring of 1863, he guided his regiment back to his old plantation at Port Royal, Virginia, and killed his former overseer.

Turner served with distinction throughout the war, fighting for a new version and a new vision of the Union and its great ennobling promise, made four score and seven years before, that all men were created equal. Now, as the war drew to its close, he moved to New England, finding work as a logger. Ultimately, he decided to settle in Vermont, because it was, he told his family, the only state admitted to the Union with slavery already proscribed. In fact, as early as 1786, the quirky, defiant, fiercely independent Republic of Vermont had passed a bill forbidding the sale of human beings, forbidding one American owning another, or their forced removal from its territory.

Alex Turner lived out his life in the gentle green hills of Grafton, Vermont, running a farm and raising a family which came to include, in 1883, a daughter, Daisy, who would in her miraculous lifetime connect the past with the present and so perpetuate that magnificent drama we call history.

Daisy Turner lived to see more than one hundred of her own years, finding as she went enough time in her busy life to give a documentary filmmaker a few minutes of priceless film poetry. Sitting blind and nearly totally deaf, in a nursing home in Springfield, Vermont, that would be her final residence, with perfect diction she flawlessly recited the dozens of rhyming couplets that make up "The Soldier's Story," a poem she had known for more than ninety years, a heart-wrenching poem about a young man's death in battle during the Civil War.

We divided her stunning recitation into five more or less equal sections and distributed them, no, sowed them like seeds, throughout our sequence on the Battle of Gettysburg. The result is that Daisy Turner became a kind of cinematic Greek chorus, rising above the terror and horror of the greatest battle ever fought in the Western Hemisphere. Daisy personalized our presentation in a way few histories have been able to do, and by so doing, reminded us all of the power of history itself.

I am interested in the "power of history," in its many varied voices and its many messages. American history is a loud, raucous, moving, exquisite collection of noises, that in the aggregate often combine to make the sweetest kind of music, and I have tried to listen to as much music as I can in putting together the Civil War series and my other films.

Too often as a culture we have ignored this joyful noise, becoming in the process blissfully ignorant of the power those past lives and stories and moments have over this moment, and indeed, our unknown future.

For many years, I hoped to do a history of the Civil War on film, but I had never been able to get up the courage. Then on Christmas Day, 1984, I finished reading a book that literally changed my life. It was a novel of the battle of Gettysburg called *The Killer Angels* and it was written by a man named Michael Shaara. It had won the Pulitzer Prize in the mid-seventies and had been recommended to me by many friends.

As I finished the book that special day, I remembered the words of the theater founder and director Tyrone Guthrie. He said, "We are looking for ideas large enough to be afraid of again." This was it. Although each of my previous films had been risky, each taking on a new or unfamiliar challenge, this new passion, to tell the whole story of the Civil War, would require all of the attention and bravery implicit in Guthrie's wonderful and, for me, always terrifying message.

The Killer Angels told the story of three of the most important days in American history; the high-water mark of the Confederacy, the mistake of all mistakes by Robert E. Lee, indeed, the price the South would have to pay for having Robert E. Lee as its general: *Gettysburg*, the greatest battle ever fought in the Western Hemisphere.

But what was important to me about the book was that it introduced me, for the first time, to Joshua Lawrence Chamberlain. And for all intents and purposes, it was the life of Chamberlain which convinced me to embark on the most difficult and satisfying experience of my life.

It is my belief that Chamberlain represents the best kind of history, the best kind of American. His is the story which always gets overlooked in the superficial aerial views of history we are usually presented with. He enlivens, though, page after page of history, as we learn first of his early life as a professor at Bowdoin, then as the green colonel of the 20th Maine, finally as a hero at Fredericksburg, Petersburg, and Gettysburg, especially Gettysburg, where on Little Round Top he executes an obscure textbook maneuver that saves the Union army and quite possibly the Union itself.

He is also a hero of another kind at Appomattox. In my view, this was *truly* his finest hour. It was a different kind of heroism there that we need so desperately to be aware of today.

Chamberlain was given the task of receiving the flags of the tattered Confederate army during the formal surrender which took place a few days after Lee and Grant had met, so poignantly in Wilmer McLean's parlor, to discuss in preliminary fashion the terms. Now, at this solemn ceremony, where Chamberlain had already forbidden his men to cheer or taunt their rebel counterparts, he made an extra-ordinary gesture. John B. Gordon, the Confederate general who had the painful task of supervising the final march of his army, saw and said it best I think, and I quote: "Chamberlain called his men into line and as my men marched in front of them, the veterans in blue gave a soldierly salute to those vanquished heroes—a token of respect from Americans to Americans." In reconciliation, Chamberlain made his greatest contribution to war.

For many years and some generations after the war, Chamberlain's story was overlooked, the actions of this citizen-hero for the most part forgotten. That is the way it is in history. Many worthwhile events and people get lost in the interpretive shuffle and it takes a new generation, a later generation, to rescue and save that which it finds important. I find Joshua Lawrence Chamberlain important. He rose to every occasion.

It is important to add that it was not all solemn and serious. Despite the great carnage he watched inflicted on his species, besides the useless death he saw, besides his own six wounds, Chamberlain still found time to record sweeter moments. A few weeks after the battle of Fredericksburg, that unmitigated disaster for the Union, Chamberlain told his brother Tom that he had never felt so well and so alive in his life, and added, "What makes it strange, is that I should have gained 12 pounds living on worms."

Humor, of course, played an important role in the Civil War, easing the pain and *relieving* the horror we were visiting on our own family members. During the long, cold, rainy winter of 1863, Confederate forces huddled in defensive positions south of the Duck River, near Tullahoma, Tennessee. Confederate officers liked to explain that Tullahoma came from the Greek words "Tulla" meaning mud, and "homa" meaning more mud.

Abraham Lincoln said if he ever saw a man homelier than himself, he'd shoot the wretch and put him out of his misery. Stonewall Jackson never ate pepper because he thought it would make his left leg ache. He rode into battle, in fact, with one arm raised, to keep, he said, the blood balanced, and he never mailed a letter if he thought it would be in transit on a Sunday. The bombastic John Pope, a terrible Union general, so often signed his dispatches "headquarters in the saddle" that Lincoln finally said Pope had his headquarters where his hindquarters ought to be. Grant said he knew only two tunes: one was Yankee Doodle and the other wasn't. And Sherman hated newspapermen so much that he said if he killed them all there would be news from Hell before breakfast.

For many of us, we are brought to our history in just this fashion. With story, memory, anecdote, feeling. These emotional connections become a kind of glue which makes the most complex of past events stick in our minds and our hearts, permanently a part of who each of us is now.

But for most of the life of this republic, the way we have *formally* told our history was from the top down. This has been called the history of the State or of great men, and it basically focuses only on presidents and wars and generals. It relies, like certain current economic policies, on an erroneous belief that this history trickles down and touches experiences common to us all. It rarely does. It does exhibit, or has exhibited, an understandable arrogance, and we have had to rely on family memory and community recollection for the good stuff. Or at least the stuff that made all that political history meaningful.

But as we have grown older as a country, as we have moved around more, lost touch with place more, these personal histories have dried up for most people, and we began to forget. History became a kind of castor oil of dry dates and facts and events of little meaning, something we knew was good for us, but hardly good tasting. History became just another subject, not the great pageant of *everything* that has come before this moment. This moment.

About twenty or thirty years ago we woke up, partially, to this problem and began to insist on relevance in our teaching of history and on a new social history that would focus on real people doing real and recognizable things. This would be history from the bottom up, not top down, and people would respond. They did not. Relevance became an excuse for not even teaching history. And the new social history became so bogged down in statistical demographics and micro-perceptions that history began to seem like the reading of the telephone book. A new arrogance replaced the old, equally understandable, but equally devastating to the national memory. Someone expressed the new tyranny quite well when they said a history of Illinois could be written without mentioning Abraham Lincoln. Something had to change. I'm pleased to report that in some ways it has. We have, as an Academy, begun to speak of a synthesis of the old and the new histories, a way to combine the best of the top-down version, still inspiring even in its "great men" addiction, with the bottom-up version, so inspiring too at times, with the million heroic acts of women, minorities, labor, ordinary people. And we have begun to use new media and new forms of expression to tell our histories, breaking the stranglehold the Academy has had on historical exchange for the last hundred years. Remember, until we adopted the German academic model at the end of the nineteenth century, our greatest historians, like Parkman and Adams, were essential amateurs, popular writers concerned with speaking to large audiences, not just a handful of colleagues unconcerned with *how* one wrote.

Listen to what Francis Parkman had to say about the historian's responsibility: "Faithfulness to the truth of history," he wrote, "involves far more than a research, however patient and scrupulous, into *special facts*. Such facts may be detailed with the most minute exactness, and yet the narrative, taken as a whole, may be un-meaning or untrue. The narrator must seek to imbue himself with the life and spirit of the time. He must study events in all their bearings, near and remote: in the character, habits, and manners of those who took part in them. He must himself be, as it were, a sharer or spectator of the action he describes."

The telling of history is a tension between Art and Science. The *Science* of History would enumerate the myriad details equally, without discrimination; the telephone book at its worst. The *Art* of History has produced *Gone With the Wind*, and worse, *The Birth of a Nation*, and recent mini-series dramas which try to convince us that it was not brother against brother, but heaving bosom against heaving bosom.

Good history has always struck a balance between these two polarities, never allowing formal considerations to overwhelm and capsize the truth of events, nor allowing a dry recitation of fact to render its meaning unintelligible or worse—boring. In an age of changing media, these dangers and pitfalls become even more critical, require even more of our vigilance and attention if we are to survive. For it is a question of survival. Without any past, certainly the current national elective, we will deprive ourselves of the defining impressions of our being.

Toward the end of the production a friend of mine at the National Archives sent me a bunch of old papers about some skirmishes in Western Virginia during the Civil War. There wasn't time to include it in our series; indeed, the old top-down version of history would not have even glanced at these old papers of campaigns long forgotten, statistical records best left unsifted. I bring them up because they have personal meaning to real people, sometimes they speak louder than the larger aerial views of the war do. Those reports included mentions of the actions of a Union general Averall in the newly created State of West Virginia at Moorefield in August of 1863. It seems that Averall was able to capture a group of Confederate cavalrymen in a small skirmish. The southerners

were mostly from Captain McClanahan's Co. of Virginia
Horse Artillery. They were, in the fascinating details of these
records, completely out-gunned. Three men were killed, five
wounded, and thirteen were made prisoners and sent to Camp
Chase in Ohio to be eventually paroled in March 1865. The
records at Camp Chase are sketchier, but they do record
receiving, processing, and releasing (paroling) the prisoners.
They are a fairly nondescript bunch. Most seem to have come
from Bathe County, Virginia. None were slaveholders, or
looked to have much interest in the Constitutional issues. One
fellow was described as being 5 feet, 4 inches tall, with a dark
complexion, gray eyes, and dark hair. He said he was a blacksmith in life and stated to the copyist, a Mr. R. W. Pearson, that
he had been forced to join the Confederate army. Another
copyist, a Mr. Jameison, places the group of "rebels" at Cox's
Wharves on the James River near City Point on March 11 or
12, 1865, where all records of the men disappear.

I was struck by the impersonal nature of the papers and yet
a sense that real Americans had lived through this war. Had
been touched by it. Fought. Were captured. Held prisoner.
Released. Shod horses. Maybe in the top-down version of
things they didn't matter much, but in someone's history they
do and that makes for a different history.

Not far from Abraham Lincoln's White House, Vaclav
Havel, the poet-president of the new Czech Republic, spoke
about the salvation of the human world. That salvation, he said,
"lies nowhere else than in the human heart, in the human
power to reflect, in human weakness and in human responsibility." Freely quoting the sixteenth President, Havel acknowledged that Lincoln too knew about the human heart and the
human world.

More than 150 years ago, in 1838, Abraham Lincoln challenged us to consider the real threat to the country, to consider forever the real cost of our inattention: "Whence shall we expect the approach of danger?" he wrote. "Shall some trans-Atlantic giant step the earth and crush us at a blow? Never. All the armies of Europe and Asia could not by force take a drink from the Ohio River or make a track in the Blue Ridge in the trial of a thousand years. No, if destruction be our lot, we must ourselves be its author and finisher. As a nation of free men, we will live forever or die by suicide." Lincoln, of course, presided over the closest this country has ever come to national suicide. This was the Civil War, our great, tragic epic story, the American *Iliad*; as relevant today as at any time in our history. It was a poignant family drama that reveals more of the American character, is more defining of us as a nation than any other event before or after.

If I said I had been working on a film series about an imperial presidency, about a growing feminist movement, about an ever present civil rights question, about greedy Wall Street speculators who stole millions trading on inside information, about unscrupulous military contractors who sold inferior goods at exorbitant prices to the government, about prying, often meddlesome and insensitive media, about new weapons capable of mass destruction on a scale previously unheard of, it would be clear that I was speaking of the present. But I am speaking of only a few issues of the American Civil War, a war that continues to speak to central questions of our present time.

It is, therefore, no accident that the best-selling nonfiction book several years ago was *Battle Cry of Freedom*, that the Hollywood movie *Glory* did so well, that the Library of America's best-selling volumes are the collected writings of Lincoln, that from editorial page to opinion page, from *Playboy* to the *New York Times*, writers are quoting and citing Lincoln, that battlefield re-enactment groups continue to grow, that dozens of books seeking to explain the war's special significance are published each year, that Hollywood plans still more films, that we have released our five-year labor of love. Each generation, Lewis Mumford once said, rediscovers and re-examines that part of the past which brings the present new meaning and new possibilities. The Civil War, like no other time in our history, now brings that special correspondence to *our* present, shocking us with its power to inform and invigorate.

I was drawn to the Civil War because it seemed to be the central influence on all the other subjects I had made films about. I assembled a first-rate team, including my brother Ric, the writer Geoffrey C. Ward, editor Paul Barnes, narrator David McCullough, the incomparable Shelby Foote—a genuine national treasure—and more than three dozen remarkable "voices"—men and women in arts and letters who read from diaries, journals, love letters, military dispatches, and newspapers that give our presentation of the war an experiential feeling.

We concerned ourselves with ordinary soldiers as well as the great politicians and generals, followed the fortunes of two towns, North and South, as well as the great battles of the war. We looked at the diplomatic struggles, the role of women, and most important, reported the true and heroic story of American blacks—not as mere passive bystanders to the struggle, but active, dedicated, self-sacrificing soldiers in an intensely personal drama of self-liberation. It is the best story I know.

Frederick Douglass, the great black statesman and passionate advocate of abolition and emancipation, and, I believe, one of the truly great men who have ever lived, indeed second only, in this Civil War period, to Abraham Lincoln, once said, "Without struggle there is no progress." When I reflect on the more than five and a half years this production took, the many obstacles met and overcome, the years of doubt and frustration that we could ever really comprehend the war, the sense that we really did bite off more than we could chew, I realize how much Douglass's fiery political statement speaks to the creative process, our process, as well.

In many ways, Douglass defines creativity. Too often, in my profession (and I suspect this is true everywhere, in many areas), too often documentary films are merely the expression of an already arrived-at end. The medium is employed only to state what is known beforehand. There is no discovery, there is no investigation. The exercise is essentially empty of meaning. Material is imposed upon, rather than listened to. The hierarchy of the production team is just that, subservient to the abstract notions of the so-called creator, prevented from influencing the project or being influenced by the interpretation of data, prisoners forever to preconception.

The great jurist Learned Hand once said that "liberty was never being too sure you're right." Another wonderful definition of creativity. One of the great lessons we learned in the course of this production was how much we had to question assumptions, doubt easy solutions, verify continually what already seemed to have worked, and constantly avoid the notion that we knew what the truth was in advance. Only the sometimes anxious state of unknowing seemed to hold the key to what would eventually end up in the finished film.

Indeed, our production was a kind of benevolent dictatorship. Until the critical moment of final decision, each player, from the bottom-rung researcher or assistant editor right up to the producer and director, had equal opportunity to influence any aspect of the production. Then the decision was mine. But now I could make it in the informed environment of a wide spectrum of options. The buck clearly stopped at my desk, the choice was ultimately mine, but because I had not exerted my will earlier, or imposed preconceptions on my material, we allowed for the widest possible team participation, and that was good for creativity.

Interestingly, we also found in the Civil War series that creativity was complexity. Too often we manipulate the facts of history to paint a simplistic, often rosy, view of what happened. We found that by lifting up the rug of history and sweeping out the dirt, we did not in any way diminish the force of our narrative. Indeed, we strengthened it. Characters like Lincoln and Lee who have been smothered in myths of perfection over the years were now real people, flawed as you and I are, but real, and that brought us closer to them and their struggles, personalizing the past like no Madison Avenue sanitized version could ever do. We learned more, retained more, and most important cared more for these men, knowing as we did of their sins as well as their virtues. It seems to me true of any endeavor, that in simplification we murder, in complexity we are faced with untidiness, to be sure, but also a good deal of truth.

But more than any one thing, creativity seemed to be attention. Attention to detail. Attention to authenticity. Attention to craft. Attention. We became in a way the Paul Masson of documentary film companies, refusing to release our project until it was finished. This of course flew in the face of established media production in this country which demands that things be produced on the fly, quickly, for immediate dissemination. When I told people that I was working on a history of the Civil War and that it would take five years to make, they were shocked. I must be wasting time. They are not shocked now. Time was the critical ingredient, only they had it backwards. Time, attention, worked for us because we were willing to allow the material, the evidence of the past, to speak to us. We listened to what it wanted, to how it wanted itself to be presented, we perched on roof-tops and at battlefields at precisely the time and day and moment the battles took place, straining not merely to get an image, any image, but to take back a little of the magic of the past.

In fact, spending the time and being free enough to allow the material to speak for itself allowed us to expand the project from the proposed five-hour, five-part series to the nine-episode, eleven-hour epic we released. The decision to expand was made well into editing, a difficult decision, but one which clearly has been supported by the reaction to the film. If we had not been open to any contingency, programmed as most shows are to just illustrate their scripts and be done with it, we would have missed an opportunity to enlarge our vision and therefore the vision of our intended audience, still another definition of creativity.

We wrote our script unconcerned with whether there were images to fill what we wanted to write about. We shot the old photographs unconcerned with whether there might be a scene in the script which these images could illustrate. In fact, we avoided illustration, preferring to take the harder, more time-consuming route of discovering the new and unique relationships that could be forged between the word and image when freed from the tyranny of doing it the quick and dirty and formulaic way. All of this liberated our filmmaking and liberated us. It allowed us to begin to tell the story of what happened during the war in a new and, for many people, vivid way, where the past, at rare but surprising dramatic moments, came alive.

But the struggle to make good history often makes for strange allies, and danger comes from unexpected and often dispiriting quarters. You have to guard your flank. When I asked Shelby Foote, in an interview for our film, what he thought about U.S. Grant, without hesitation he said, "Grant had what you call four o'clock in the morning courage. That means you could wake him up at four in the morning to tell him that the enemy had turned his right flank and he'd be as cool as a cucumber. That's four o'clock in the morning courage."

Our production required large doses of four o'clock in the morning courage, and sometimes the attack came from unexpected parties. Early in the production, four years before our scheduled broadcast, our principal writer, Geoffrey C. Ward, delivered a preliminary first draft of a script. We decided to assemble our distinguished body of historical advisers, nearly two dozen in number when we first started out, for a script review session. These consultants ranged from conservative, one might say, Confederate historians, chroniclers of the Lost Cause, all the way to Marxist historians who argued quite eloquently that the only important story of the Civil War was emancipation, the struggles in Congress, and the social transformation that the war and emancipation fostered across the land.

We, as filmmakers, had no set agenda. We felt that slavery was bad, George McClellan timid, but that the rest of the war, North and South, male and female, black and white, civilian and military, was a vast and complicated family drama, poetic as well as social in dimension, emotional as well as didactic in context and scope, instructive to the heart as well as the head. We felt that film, despite its apparent superficial qualities, had the ability to synthesize and unite diverse perspectives and it was our intention to include in our series the pain and violence of slavery along with the catastrophic loss of human life in battle. We sought to feel the grief of mothers from all sides of the conflict and we sought to understand the disparity of character in individuals as flamboyant as Nathan Bedford Forrest, Benjamin Butler, and Stonewall Jackson. We sought to learn what actually happened in certain battles dismissed by our own teachers as irrelevant to the more important causes and effects of the war, because we felt that American life mattered and that the outcome of these struggles, more then most wars, mattered to all Americans today. More than anything, we knew that we did not know everything, that we wished to learn from our distinguished colleagues.

For a day it worked. Our script was roundly criticized as missing many elements, which we ourselves advertised, but on the whole it was a superb first draft, everyone felt. On the second day, new historians arrived and the tone quickly changed. Most of these historians, closer to our own political hearts than they will ever know or believe, were those who felt our first draft to be woefully lacking in elements which would illuminate this struggle for emancipation. Try as we might, we could not convince these well-meaning people that we were only beginning the process of writing, that we had asked them there to add exactly what they said was missing, and that the process of filmmaking necessitated our committing to a rough simplistic structure until further additions, hopefully added by them and others, could enrich our relatively feeble first steps. After all, that's why they were there.

The "new" historians were not convinced. For several hours they argued quite spitefully and belligerently, as if this early draft was the way it was going to turn out. In fact, it was the first of nearly twenty complete revisions. We pleaded and protested, insisted that we were corrigible, begged them to tell us what was missing, to no avail. It was a dark moment, requiring four o'clock in the morning courage. We had been attacked on our flank by those we considered our allies and it hurt.

Finally, C. Vann Woodward, the great historian, who had been with us both days, and who had sat quietly through much of this rather embarrassing exchange, looked at me and riveted the attention of everyone in the room, including the angry historians, many of whom were his former students. After a long silence he spoke: "Ken, we pedants hope that we don't get in the way of your telling this story well. What is it that we can do to help you tell this story better?" From that moment on, we had every one's help, some less begrudgingly offered than others, and we were actually able to put into the final version of our film nearly every one of the suggestions those doubting historians wanted. (Later on, during our lunch break, I met Woodward in the hall outside the meeting room and immediately brevetted him Major-General in the field for his bravery and courage in protecting our flank. To this day, we still refer to each other as General Woodward and General Burns.)

We hoped that that would be it. We worked hard for four more years on the project and when it was released, 98 percent of the letters and criticism was overwhelmingly positive. One percent, we discovered, felt we had slighted the South, one percent thought we were too sympathetic to the South, including a few of the historians we had worked with that first review day and throughout the production.

Most galling, however, was the celebrated historian who first called me to congratulate me on a "superb and wonderful" film, especially on the causes of the war, and who later criticized the film gratuitously in a review of an unrelated scholarly work on the war. It seemed to me an indication of an almost lock-step mentality among those who looked through our stark and devastating portrait of the reality of slavery and the experience of black troops in the war, who ignored the majority of our series which was not about battle but about the myriad changes in American society (South as well as North), and saw only capitulation to an "old" narrative pro-southern version of history.

Never had we said that our film version of the war was the only version. Never had we said that it was a comprehensive view of the war. Indeed, our earliest proposal indicated our sense of any film's fragile capacity for complexity and we urged early on a tolerant understanding of its true visceral attributes: the ability to make you feel. We had even gone so far as to admit the many scenes that had been excised due to the editing's subtle dictates. We said out loud many times we wished for this section and that section to be expanded, that more could have been done on this moment and more could have been done on that moment, but because of our medium, with all its inherent strengths and weaknesses, because of the almost Aristotelian demands of structure and pacing, our film, not theirs, *looked this way*. We were proud of our work, but saddened by the vitriol emanating from those with whom we felt such intellectual kinship.

Which is to say we were not prepared for the attack on our credibility that came from those so close to our own sensibilities. Were they jealous, as many suggested, of the film's great popularity? Had they been left on the cutting-room floor? Had they been promised to be interviewed and then not been? Had we failed to subscribe solely to their accepted school of thought, daring to combine and interweave a variety of approaches and perspectives? Had they forgotten the difference between literary scholarship and the demands of a popular medium? Hadn't their own books done well after the broadcast as bookstores across the country expanded their Civil War sections? Hadn't the experience on the whole been a positive one, prompting lively debate, free exchange, initiating new programs on specific aspects of the war, and generally uniting, if briefly, a country whose edges had frayed more than usual?

It was a difficult passage for those of us who worked on the film, but nothing compared with trying to find a way to make that defining conflict real.

At 4:30 a.m. on the 12th of April, 1861, General Pierre Gustave Toutant Beauregard directed his Confederate gunners to open fire on Fort Sumter, at that hour only a dark shape out in Charleston harbor. Thirty-four hours later a white flag over the fort ended the bombardment. The only casualty was a Confederate horse. It was a bloodless opening to the bloodiest war in American history.

No one could have predicted the magnitude of the explosion that rocked America following that opening shot. Until then America had been, as Bruce Catton wrote, "small enough to carry in the mind and in the heart, and a young man's fatherland was what he could see from his bedroom window." Yet most of what America was before the Civil War went into sparking that explosion and most of what it became resulted from it. Entirely unimaginable before it began, the war was the most defining and shaping event in American history—so much so that it is now impossible to imagine what we would have been like without it.

Shortly after Appomattox, Walt Whitman, a Brooklyn journalist and sometime poet who worked in the appalling Union hospitals, warned posterity of what he had seen. "Future years," he wrote, "will never know the seething hell and the black infernal background, the countless minor scenes and interiors of the secession war; and it is best they should not. The real war," Whitman insisted, "will never get in the books."

The writers and historians of future years were not scared off by Whitman's admonition. In a century and a quarter following the War's conclusion, more than fifty thousand books were published on the Civil War: countless personal diaries and regimental histories, biographies and military narratives, pictorial essays, social analyses, works that have treated causes and effects, demographics, crop statistics, even the weather. There have been books of maps, books of letters, books of orders, books of books, slim philosophical essays and three-volume narratives, novels, poems, and music. Each year dozens of new titles appear, again offering to revisit the war, to reinterpret or rearrange those strange days and hard events—faint traces and distant signals now—looking still for the coherent, the conclusive explanation.

And yet Whitman's words retain their force. The "real war" stays there, outside all the books, beckoning to us. Why did Americans kill each other and how did it happen? Who *were* these people who fought and killed, marched and sang, wrote home, skedaddled, deserted, died, nursed and lamented, persevered and were defeated? What was it like to be in that war? What did it do to America and Americans? What happened to the movement that freed blacks from slavery? Why have succeeding generations obscured the war with bloodless, gallant myth, blurring the causes and its great ennobling outcome— the freeing of four million black people and their descendants from bondage? What did it mean that the Union won? What does it mean to be a Union? Why are we still so drawn to this tale of suffering, catastrophe, heroism, and death? These were the questions we asked.

In the past fifteen years I have learned many things, but that history is our greatest teacher is perhaps the most important lesson. This enthusiasm, however, is by no means shared by all. History and its valuable counsel continue to recede in importance and emphasis in schools across the land. The statistics are now very frightening. A majority of high school seniors do not know who Joseph Stalin or Winston Churchill were. They did not know, of the Emancipation Proclamation, the Bill of Rights, and the Declaration of Independence, which came first. Many thought we fought with the Germans against the Russians in the Second World War. And a majority could not tell the correct half-century in which the Civil War took place.

Why *do* we forget? Who and What are to blame? Well, film and television mostly. Television is rapidly eroding the strength of our republic from within (just as Lincoln predicted); substituting a distracting cultural monarchy for the diversity and variety and democracy promised in its conception and unveiling. Instead of dozens of options on the tube, we now see nearly the same thing everywhere, always presented the same way, on dozens of clone-like channels. Television has equipped us as citizens to live only in all-consuming, and thereby forgettable and disposable, present, blissfully unaware of the historical tides and movements that speak not only to this moment, but to our vast future as well. This environment ensures that we have no *history*. And by so doing, ensures that we have no *future*.

Even supposedly enlightened shows do more harm than good, wind up serving the same Morphean end, by conferring a kind of cultural peerage on the familiar talking heads that appear and reappear with striking sameness each night. Issues and ideas are merely pushed around the plate—never digested—by the same people, *always* the same people, engaged more with a subtle one-upmanship among themselves and their TV alter egos than with the advancement of our understanding. In the worst of our television, we are addicted to personality, to the breathless embrace of celebrity, ensuring as we go a tyranny of the televised over the great mass of the untelevised. There can be no communication in this world except among equals, and how do we convince *our monster* to confer on us the intelligence we have. (Except for rare moments of great national trauma and in the form-transcending moments of pure sport, like baseball, television confers nothing in return but a potentially lethal light in our living rooms and minds.)

Even the best of those in television, and that includes all of us in public television, get caught up in near constant self-congratulation about their role in the medium, in near constant self-righteous invocation of shadowy "chilling effects" and influences that would limit their Constitutionally initiated rights, but always forgetting to stress to themselves and their audience how much the medium must improve, how little of its brain it actually uses, how by striving for a superficial ideal of balance it has ensured mediocrity, by its almost comic unearthing of simplistic villains, it has forgotten to select for heroes.

Television can remind us too, if we let it. We know the horrible statistics about television, how it divides us, encourages us to see ourselves as economic units rather than as spiritual beings, as Vartan Gregorian, the president of Brown University, says. But we mustn't throw the medium out, turn away, or surrender its great power to those disingenuous people for whom it is merely the tool of some temporal or financial end. It is not enough to blame it all on television. Lincoln, in 1862, forced to place George McClellan, a slow, timid, but experienced general back in charge of his humiliated army, said, "We must use the tools we have."

Let us use these tools now. As we gradually become a country and a society without letter-writing and diary-keeping, more and more dependent on visual signs and language, television will become more and more an important part of the making of history. More and more we will be connected to the past by the images we have made, and *they* will become the glue that makes memories.

Eventually, television will, I suggest, become our new Homeric form (told around an electronic campfire), the way we can and must speak to succeeding generations. It seems too easy to dismiss its cruder aspects, to turn away from its clearly manipulative elements, or cave in to its seductive power. We must learn how to use it, make it speak our truths and tell our stories, our his-stories, in an honorable fashion.

I must confess, however, on Sunday, September 23, 1990, we had no idea what to expect of our small attempt at historical enlightenment and our very large demand on the attention of the country. That morning I checked out of a hotel in midtown Manhattan, after more than two months on the road, trying to drum up support for what everyone agreed was an extremely risky experiment: running *The Civil War* for five consecutive nights during the height of the new commercial fall season. As I made the long trip home, sure the coming week would be a calm reprieve, the comments of several columnists who were sure that we would be "eaten alive" by the networks kept echoing in my mind. We were all, therefore, completely unprepared for what was to happen to our lives.

Within minutes of the first night's broadcast, the phone began ringing off the hook with calls from across the country, eager to find out about Sullivan Ballou, anxious to learn the name of Jay Ungar's superb theme music "Ashokan Farewell," desperate to share their families' experience in the war or just kind enough to say thanks. The calls would not stop all week—and they continue still five years later. The series was the highest rated show in the history of Public Television, drawing an incredible 39 million people for its first viewing.

Now we are recognized throughout the country—in stores, in airports, on city streets. Shelby Foote, rightfully so, has become a revered household name, even a sex symbol. We've become *New Yorker* cartoons and National Public Radio spoofs, and *Saturday Night Live* skits. *Twin Peaks* worked *The Civil War* into its bizarre plot for several weeks. *The Tonight Show* called and we answered. Book signings sell out of our high-priced companion book in minutes. The television series *Thirtysomething* put *The Civil War* into an episode one Christmas—they should call it, I suppose, *130 Something*. Reporters still call night and day, persistently finding new angles to keep the story alive, trying to figure out why, a century and a quarter later, the Civil War continues to speak to us in a clear voice.

And the effect has gone even deeper into our culture. Churches across the country now play "Ashokan Farewell" regularly at services; at a funeral for a young man in Vidalia, Louisiana, Sullivan Ballou's letter to Sarah was read. We are constantly stopped by people who say their lives have been permanently changed by *The Civil War* series. And the thousands of letters we have received belie the oft-stated assumption that we Americans no longer know how to write. These letters are beautiful, touching, *attentive* expressions of very deep and complex emotions, not dissimilar to Major Ballou's. That is truly good news.

To my surprise and delight, the eloquence of the common man that we had worked so hard to put in our film came through in thousands of new letters from Americans who were supposed to be completely numbed by television and a postmodern age that had lulled them to blissful, ignorant sleep.

One man from Oregon wrote, "I am left with an odd assortment of emotions, that out of such utter horror so much bravery and courage could be displayed, as to make us feel a sense of pride in those terrible events. I mostly feel a longing for the simplicity of conviction felt by so many of those men and women, uncluttered by the confusion of today's society."

For a Canadian from Ontario, the series and what he learned of the Civil War finally made him understand his complicated neighbor to the south. What had infuriated him about us before, he now understood. "The trouble with most wars," he writes, "is that 'the enemy' is mysterious and inscrutable and therefore menacing . . . But both sides in the Civil War were equally human and understandable . . . I do not know whether we Canadians are fortunate in not having such a terrible event in our history . . . *The Civil War* has been a poignant emotional experience for me over my lifetime. But I can say with the deepest sincerity that I share your sorrow and exultation as you look on your country's bloody and yet inspiring past."

For others, their response is even more personal, almost religious. A man from Franklinton, North Carolina, writes, "It is now two days after my experience of the Civil War has ended and my life remains changed. . . . I have been aware of an opening in my soul that I could not understand—a confrontation with certain truths about myself and my country that up until this week I could not rationalize. I now realize that the pangs I've felt are those of an *American*. That deep in my soul the Civil War is alive."

A woman from upstate New York shared our belief that the Civil War was our great, epic, Homeric poem of national self-definition. "I watched with a puzzling sense of recurring memory until I recognized [the series] as an American *Bhagavad Gita*, with its paradox of love and conflict, genius and ignorance, and finally the human transcendence that may one day show us where the real battles need to be fought, quite apart from geography. I look at present times from a different place now . . . ."

Thanks to a supplementary educational package produced by one of our underwriters, General Motors, schools across the country are now showing the series in class. We've received more than 6000 letters and cards from secondary school teachers alone, grateful for the series, pleased with how well it works as a teaching tool. Recently we received a pack of letters from nearly thirty fourth- and fifth-graders at a school in Austin, Minnesota. Because the children were so young, their teachers showed them only a few minutes of the series at a time, but gradually from October to May, they saw the entire eleven hours. "I think I'll remember this movie for a long time," one young girl wrote, "it touched, touched and warmed the hearts of almost every person that watched it including me myself." Another wrote: "The Civil War is very hard to believe. How could America go to war against itself? How could anyone kill another of his or her own kind? It was tragic."

In December 1991 I received the most interesting letter. It came from a soldier stationed in Arabia. This young sergeant's great-great-grandfather had ridden with Lee and Jackson and Gordon. He believed that his own developing religious faith had been born in an appreciation of his ancestor's actions during the Civil War. He himself had been recently baptized in the Appomattox River not far from the surrender site—a surrender of a different kind, he noted. "My love for history is hard to put into words," he admitted. "I still feel I have a destiny to fulfill in working with preserving our national heritage. . . ." His letter ends most extraordinarily: "Last Christmas I stood in Noriega's office, his dress hat is one of my proud possessions. Now I'm in this desert, war may come soon. Nothing is more incredible than being a witness to history. Please pray for U.S." (I'm pleased to say he made it through the war.)

Recently, I received a stunning letter which may be the most profound of all.

> Dear Sir:
>
> Again, I am watching *The Civil War*—enthralled, inspired, heartbroken. So much to think about, so much to feel:
>
> The eloquence of ordinary people resounds. It humbles me.
>
> Such dignity in the archival faces of my people, who were enslaved, but who never surrendered their souls to slavery.
>
> I hear the Southerners who not only kept my ancestors in bondage, but fought to the death to do so. And I hate them for that.
>
> Then the choir sings: "Do you . . . do you . . . want your freedom?" A good question, for we are not yet truly free, none of us.

To achieve that, white America must abandon its racial conceits—and I must abandon my hate. They must change, and I must forgive, for us both to be free.

Lincoln was right. "Malice toward none, charity for all."

So at the end, I wonder. Does my white counterpart, hearing that choir, realize that that final question is meant for both of us?

"Do you . . . do you . . . want your freedom?"

I know what my answer is. I will wait for his.

The most moving letter we received was from a young widow in Ohio. Her husband had been killed in a tragic accident a few days after the series ran, leaving four young children fatherless. One of the last things she and her beloved husband had done together was to watch *The Civil War*. She writes, "I am so grateful for the time it gave us together. . . . We shared those nights our feelings about history, war, life and death. Upon hearing the reading of Sullivan Ballou's letter, my husband simply looked my way, smiled and said, 'that just about says it all . . .' I requested that the Sullivan Ballou letter be read to the standing room only crowd [at his funeral]. What resulted was a celebration of what a positive impact our lives—and deaths—can have. No words can truly capture my loss and my fear. On a number of occasions, when I have felt too weary to carry on, I remember the courage of the men and women you so beautifully and eloquently shared with us."

The series has touched a chord which is still vibrating and will continue to vibrate as long as the Republic lives. If you see the history of a country in the same sympathetic personal way you see the life of a human being, then it is clear that the Civil War was the great traumatic event in the childhood of this nation. Disguise it as we may, ignore it as we usually do, distort it as we have so often done, we cannot ultimately not be continually influenced by this terrible terrible memory of the four years during which we came close to ending our national life.

My own mother died when I was eleven, changing me and permanently influencing all that I would become. The Civil War defines us in just that way, at both an intensely intimate level and in a broad national sense. And as Barbara Fields, the Columbia University historian, reminds us in the series, in calling to mind the plight of the homeless and the larger disparities between people based on class and race, "The Civil War is still going on. It's still to be fought and regrettably it can still be lost."

Finally, Lincoln, of course, said it best. Early in 1861, at his first inauguration, when he still hoped to keep his country together, he implored southerners not to go to war. "We must not be enemies," he said. "We *must* be friends." But then he went on, "The mystic chords of memory, stretching from every battle-field and patriot grave, to every living heart and hearthstone, all over this broad land, will yet swell the chorus of the Union, when again touched, as surely they will be by the better angels of our nature."

Speaking of memory. That Confederate blacksmith who was captured at Moorefield, West Virginia, and imprisoned at Camp Chase in Ohio was named Abraham Burns—my great-great-grandfather.

Notes

1. Help From Historians

1. Ken Burns and Ric Burns in the "Introduction" to Geoffrey C. Ward with Ric Burns and Ken Burns, *The Civil War: An Illustrated History* (New York, 1990), xvii.

2. Ken Burns, "Speech for Civil War Institute," Gettysburg, Pennsylvania, June 28, 1991 (MS), p. 30.

3. C. Vann Woodward to Ken Burns, January 16, 1986, from correspondence in the author's personal files—as are subsequent quotations from correspondence between myself and Burns.

4. Ric Burns to C.V.W., February 21, 1986.

5. Ken Burns to C.V.W., July 11, 1986.

6. Ric Burns to C.V.W., October 9, 1987.

7. Ken Burns to C.V.W., April 25, 1990.

8. C.V.W. to Ken Burns, November 2, 1988.

9. Don E. Fehrenbacher to Ken Burns, November 2, 1988. This letter and the next three quoted are in the Burns files.

10. Shelby Foote to Ken Burns, November 13, 1988.

11. William S. McFeely to Ken Burns, November 17, 1988.

12. C.V.W. to Ken Burns, November 2, 1988.

2. *Ken Burns's* The Civil War *as an Interpretation of History*

1. Edward Hazlett Carr, *What Is History?* (New York, 1965), 36–69.

2. Good excerpts representative of these positions can be found in Edwin C. Rozwenc, *The Causes of the American Civil War* (Boston, 1961). See, particularly, Avery Craven, "The Breakdown of the Democratic Process," 171–80, and James G. Randall, "The Blundering Generation," 163–70.

3. Arthur Schlesinger, Jr., "The Causes of the American Civil War: A Note on Historical Sentimentalism," *Partisan Review*, XVI (1949):968–81.

4. Gunnar Myrdal, *An American Dilemma: The Negro Problem and Modern Democracy* (New York and London, 1944).

5. Allan Nevins, *The Ordeal of the Union*, Vols. I and II (New York, 1947).

6. Robert Bren· Toplin's interview with Ken Burns, Summer, 1990.

7. James M. McPherson, *Battle Cry of Freedom: The Civil War Era* (New York, 1988); Richard H. Sewell, *Ballots for Freedom: Antislavery Politics in the United States, 1837–1860* (New York, 1976); Richard H. Sewell, *A House Divided: Sectionalism and Civil War* (Baltimore, 1988); David M. Potter, *Lincoln and His Party in the Secession Crisis* (New Haven, 1942); David M. Potter, *The Impending Crisis: 1848–1861* (New York, 1976); William J. Cooper, Jr., *The South and the Politics of Slavery, 1828–1856* (Baton Rouge, 1978); William J. Cooper, Jr., *Liberty and Slavery: Southern Politics to 1860* (New York, 1983).

8. Kenneth M. Stampp, *The Peculiar Institution: Slavery in the Ante-Bellum South* (New York, 1956); John Blassingame, *The Slave Community: Plantation Life in the Antebellum South* (New York, 1972).

9. David Herbert Donald, *Why the North Won the Civil War* (Baton Rouge, 1960), 112.

10. Toplin's interview with Ken Burns.

3. *How Familiarity Bred Success*

1. "Revisiting the Civil War," *Newsweek* 106 (October 8, 1990): 58–59; John E. Stanchak, "A Big War on a Small Screen," *Civil War Times Illustrated* 29 (October 1990):50–51; Gregg Biggs, "Audio/Video Reviews," *Blue & Gray Magazine* 8 (December 1990):42.

2. Daniel J. Walkowitz, "Telling the Story: The Media, the Public, and American History," *Perspectives* 31 (October 1993):1, 6–7; Ellen

Carol DuBois's review of *The Civil War*, in *The American Historical Review* 96 (October 1991):1141.

3. The professor who criticized Burns's detractors was Gordon Zimmerman of the University of Nevada, whose comments appeared as a letter to the editors in *Newsweek* 106 (October 29, 1990):14.

4. The book that accompanied the documentary, *The Civil War: An Illustrated History*, by Geoffrey C. Ward, Ric Burns, and Ken Burns (New York, 1990), follows an almost identical interpretive path.

5. On this question, see chapter 12 of James M. McPherson, *Ordeal by Fire: The Civil War and Reconstruction* (New York, 1982); chapter 10 of McPherson, *Battle Cry of Freedom: The Civil War Era* (New York, 1988); and chapter 1 of Herman Hattaway and Archer Jones, *How the North Won: A Military History of the Civil War* (Urbana, 1982).

6. Jubal A. Early, *The Campaigns of Gen. Robert E. Lee. An Address by Lieut. General Jubal A. Early, Before Washington and Lee University, January 19th, 1872* (Baltimore, 1872), 39–40; Lee's quotation is from General Orders No. 9, the text of which is reproduced in Douglas Southall Freeman, *R. E. Lee: A Biography*, 4 vols. (New York, 1934–35), 4:154–55. On Lost Cause writers who pointed to northern resources to explain defeat, see chapter 2 of Thomas L. Connelly, *The Marble Man: Robert E. Lee and His Image in American Society* (New York, 1977), and chapter 4 of Gaines M. Foster, *Ghosts of the Confederacy: Defeat, the Lost Cause, and the Emergence of the New South* (New York, 1987).

7. Thomas L. Livermore's *Numbers and Losses in the Civil War in America: 1861–65* (1900; reprint, Bloomington, 1957), the standard work on the subject, places Lee's total engaged strength during the Seven Days at 95,481 (p. 86). In *To the Gates of Richmond: The Peninsula Campaign* (New York, 1992), 156, Stephen W. Sears, who acted as a consultant to Burns, puts the number at 92,400 men.

8. Grady McWhiney and Perry D. Jamieson, *Attack and Die: Civil War Military Tactics and the Southern Heritage* (University, Ala.: 1982), 48–58 (quotation on p. 58). Edward Hagerman, *The American Civil War and the Origins of Modern Warfare: Ideas, Organization, and Field Command* (Bloomington, 1988), 16–20, also discusses antebellum efforts to adjust to rifled weaponry.

9. For a more detailed discussion of the relative importance of the Eastern and Western theaters, see Gary W. Gallagher, "'Upon Their Success Hang Momentous Issues': Generalship," in Gabor S. Boritt, ed., *Why the Confederacy Lost* (New York, 1992), 90–107.

10. Studies that argue for the primacy of the Western Theater include Thomas L. Connelly and Archer Jones, *The Politics of Command: Factions*

and Ideas in Confederate Strategy (Baton Rouge, 1973), Richard M. McMurry, *Two Great Rebel Armies: An Essay in Confederate Military History* (Chapel Hill, 1989), and Hattaway and Jones, *How the North Won*.

11. Abraham Lincoln to Henry W. Halleck, July 7, 1863, in *The Collected Works of Abraham Lincoln*, ed. Roy P. Basler and others, 9 vols. (New Brunswick, N.J., 1953), 6:319; McPherson, *Ordeal by Fire*, 333.

12. In *The Civil War: A Narrative*, 3 vols. (New York: Random House, 1958–74), Foote devotes ten pages to Pea Ridge and nearly seventy to the Red River Campaign.

13. The back cover of a recent paperback edition of *The Killer Angels* contains a quotation by Burns that leaves no doubt about his debt to Shaara: "A book that changed my life. . . . I had never visited Gettysburg, knew almost nothing about the battle before I read the book, but here it all came alive." Michael Shaara, *The Killer Angels* (New York, 1993 [38th printing]).

14. Alan T. Nolan's *Lee Considered: General Robert E. Lee and Civil War History* (Chapel Hill, 1991) sparked controversy by questioning many of the traditional assumptions about Lee that Burns accepted.

15. For negative assessments of Lee's strategic ability, see chapter 3 of Connelly and Jones, *Politics of Command*, and chapter 4 of Nolan, *Lee Considered*; for a response to Lee's critics that summarizes the principal arguments on both sides, see Gallagher, "'Upon Their Success Hang Momentous Issues': Generalship," in *Why the Confederacy Lost*.

16. James Harrison Wilson, *Under the Old Flag: Recollections of Military Operations in the War for the Union, the Spanish War, the Boxer Rebellion, Etc.*, 2 vols. (New York, 1912), 2:17; William Tecumseh Sherman to Ulysses S. Grant, March 10, 1864, printed in *Memoirs of General W. T. Sherman*, ed. Charles Royster (New York, 1990), 428.

17. U.S. War Department, *The War of the Rebellion: A Compilation of the Official Records of the Union and Confederate Armies*, 127 vols., index, and atlas (Washington: GPO, 1880–1901), Series I, vol. 43, pt. 1:917. For good discussions of Grant and Sherman, see chapter 5 of Joseph T. Glatthaar, *Partners in Command: The Relationships Between Leaders in the Civil War* (New York, 1994), and Hattaway and Jones, *How the North Won*, 686–87.

18. The quotations by Grant and Sherman are in Hattaway and Jones, *How the North Won*, 150.

19. James Ramage's *Rebel Raider: The Life of General John Hunt Morgan* (Lexington, 1986), as well as contemporary southern newspapers, letters, and diaries, strongly suggest that Morgan probably eclipsed Forrest during the war as a Confederate hero.

20. A succinct discussion of the political dimension of Pope's conduct in Virginia is in McPherson, *Battle Cry of Freedom*, 501–2; Mark Grimsley

provides a more detailed examination in "Conciliation and Its Failure, 1861–1862," *Civil War History* 39 (December 1993):317–36. Richard M. McMurry, *John Bell Hood and the War for Southern Independence* (Lexington, 1982), 116–23, and Thomas L. Connelly, *Autumn of Glory: The Army of Tennessee, 1862–1865* (Baton Rouge, 1971), 399–425, offer perceptive analyses of Johnston's removal from command of the Army of Tennessee.

4. *"Noble Women as Well"*

1. And perhaps here we see the value of constructive criticism, because Burns, wounded by charges of racial insensitivity in *The Civil War*, has been universally lauded for his expansive treatment of race and his iconographic focus on Jackie Robinson in his new eighteen-hour-plus epic on the great American pastime, *Baseball*.

2. See essays by Eric Foner and Leon Litwak in this volume.

3. I want to commend the producer of a documentary for the series *Civil War Journal* (Arts and Entertainment Network), who had not five years but less than five months to put together a program entitled *Women at War*. Laura Verklan managed to weave talking heads, compelling images, and thoughtful narration in a program that informed and illuminated.

4. I prefer to think this appellation was subliminally tied to his *Baseball* project and his fondness for the Simpsons' *paterfamilias*.

5. I regret it is so self-serving and ironic for me to trash Burns on the topic of his egregious and blatant neglect of women, as two of my last three books were shaped to deal with the topic of women and the Civil War: *Divided Houses: Gender and the Civil War* (co-edited with Nina Silber) and *Tara Revisited: Women, War and the Plantation Legend*. But after being drafted, it is *not* a tough job, and somebody's got to do it.

6. Of course, some women are granted *honorary* status, especially if they take on the role of gender policing. More likely, "NO FEMINISTS ALLOWED," and all the better if a woman can be found to advocate this position.

7. This was the subtitle of a talk I gave to interpreters of historical sites for the National Park Service. They were concerned about visitors to historical landmarks. Increasingly, families who visit historical sights to recover their national history are disappointed to find only depictions of male exploits with little evidence of any female presence or activities on display.

8. *Women and War*, produced by Laura Verklan, *Civil War Journal*.

9. Mary Vaughn to her sister, February 22, 1862, Sunnyside, Boddie Family Papers, Mississippi State Archives.

10. Charles East, ed., *Civil War Diary of Sarah Morgan* (Athens, Ga., 1991).

11. Lauren Cook Burgess, ed., *An Uncommon Soldier: The Civil War Letters of Sarah Rosetta Wakeman, alias Private Lyons Wakeman, 153rd Regiment, New York State Volunteers* (Pasadena, Md., 1994), 71.

12. *Women and War*, produced by Laura Verklan, *Civil War Journal.*

13. James McPherson, "Foreword," in Burgess, ed., *An Uncommon Soldier*, xii.

14. Bell Wiley, *Life of Johnnie Reb: The Common Soldier of the Confederacy* (Indianapolis, 1943), 55.

15. *Women and War*, produced by Laura Verklan, *Civil War Journal.*

16. Catherine Clinton, *Tara Revisited: Women, War and the Plantation Legend* (New York, 1995), 87.

17. Stephen Oates, *Woman of Valor* (New York, 1994).

18. Mary Massey, *Bonnet Brigades: American Women in the Civil War* (New York, 1966).

19. Fannie Beers, *Memories: A Record of Experiences During Four Years of War* (Philadelphia, 1891), 117.

20. Katharine Jones, ed., *Heroines of Dixie* (Indianapolis, 1955), 110.

21. L. Selina Johnson, "One Story of the Civil War: The Second Battle of Bull Run" (1898), Manuscript Collection, United Daughters of the Confederacy Headquarters, Richmond, Va.

22. Kristie Ross, "Arranging a Doll's House: Refined Women as Union Nurses," *Divided Houses: Gender and the Civil War*, Catherine Clinton and Nina Silber, eds. (New York, 1992), 108.

23. Clinton, *Tara Revisited*, 72.

24. *Ibid.*, 72–73.

25. *Ibid.*, 73–74.

26. *Ibid.*, 74.

27. Peter Bardaglio, "The Children of Jubilee," in *Divided Houses*, 221.

28. *Ibid.*, 225.

29. Jones, ed., *Heroines of Dixie*, 350.

30. Katie Miller to her aunt, April 3, 1864, French Camp, Boddie Family Papers, Mississippi State Archives.

31. Louisa Henry to her mother, March 28, 1864, Arcadia, Boddie Family Papers, Mississippi State Archives.

32. Matthew Page Andrews, *The Women in the South in Wartime* (Baltimore, 1927), 127.

33. Clinton, *Tara Revisited*, 158.

34. Indeed, no black women were included in Burns's summation program tracing lives after the war. Only a handful of blacks and women combined made this select circle.

35. Clinton, *Tara Revisited*, 103.
36. *Ibid.*
37. *Ibid.*, 104.

5. Lincoln and Gettysburg

The author is indebted to *Pennsylvania History* for permission to use here some passages from his review of the PBS series.

1. Wilson quoted in Jack Temple Kirby, *Media-Made Dixie: The South in the American Imagination* (Athens, 1986), 4.

2. Conversations with Neil Mahrer, Executive Vice President, PBS, January 17, and February 9, 1991.

3. Numerous conversations in person as well as on the telephone with Ken Burns during, Spring, 1991, and Colin Powell in person in Autumn, 1992. See also, for example, *Washington Post*, September 19, October 16, 1990; *New York Times*, September 24, 1990.

4. *Southern Partisan*. Third Quarter, 1990, p. 37. See also for example New Orleans *Times-Picayune*, Sept. 22, 1990; Alan Patureau, "Charges of Bias in Civil War Series Open Old Wounds," *Atlanta Journal and Constitution*, Sept. 22, 1990; W. Spears, "Battle Lines Drawn Over 'Civil War,'" *Philadelphia Inquirer*, Sept. 22, 1990; Jay Arnold (Associated Press), "PBS Series 'The Civil War' is Accused of Northern Bias," *Tucson Citizen*, Sept. 22, 1990; "South Fears Slam from Civil War Miniseries," Harrisburg *Patriot*, Sept. 22, 1990; "A Southern View," Augusta, Ga., *Chronicle*, Sept. 23, 1990; David Braaten, "True Sons of the South Smell a Yankee TV Plot," *Washington Times*, Sept. 25, 1990; Philip Hosmer, "Civil War Still Evokes Controversy," Bridgewater, N.J., *Courier News*, Sept. 26, 1990; "Documentary by Ken Burns," *Society of Civil War Historians Newsletter*, Sept. 1990, pp. 2–9; "Southern Group Criticizes 'Civil War,'" *Electronic Media*, October 1, 1990; "The Civil War," *U.S. News and World Report*, Oct. 8, 1990; "'Civil War' Deserves Emmy for Pseudohistory," Letter of Elizabeth Gardner Waddington, *New York Times*, Oct. 14, 1990; Ludwell Johnson, "PBS's Civil War: The Mythmanagement of History," *Southern Partisan*, Third Quarter, 1990, pp. 35–37.

The documentary was also charged with a pro-southern white and anti-black bias and this viewpoint, originating in academia, and only touched on in the media, is covered elsewhere in this book.

5. Even as this is being written, William Marvel's Lincoln Prize-winning study, *Andersonville: The Last Depot* (Chapel Hill, 1994), is revising our understanding of the subject. Footnotes here will point readers toward the best works on a question under discussion, even when they postdate the film and were not available to its creators. For a useful recent

look at history on film, including a bibliography, see John E. O'Connor, ed., *Images of Film and Television* (American Historical Association, Malabor, Fla., 1990).

6. See, for example, William A. Frassanito, *Gettysburg: A Journey in Time* (New York, 1975); Alan Trachtenberg, *Reading American Photographs: Images as History, Mathew Brady to Walker Evans* (New York, 1989); and Timothy Sweet, *Traces of War: Poetry, Photography, and the Crisis of the Union* (Baltimore, 1990).

7. Edmund Rostand, *Cyrano de Bergerac*.

8. The best book on the subject is Harry W. Pfanz, *Gettysburg: Culp's Hill and Cemetery Hill* (Chapel Hill, 1993). For a book that emphasizes the divergence of evidence and the possibilities for various interpretations, see Gabor S. Boritt, ed., *The Gettysburg Nobody Knows* (New York, forthcoming).

9. "Report of Col. Joshua L. Chamberlain, July 6, 1863," *The War of the Rebellion: A Compilation of the Official Records of the Union and Confederate Armies*, 127 vols., index, and atlas (Washington: GPO, 1880–1901), series 1, vol. 27, pt. 1, 622–26; and "Through Blood and Fire at Gettysburg," *Hearst's Magazine*, 23 (June, 1913); John J. Pullen, *The Twentieth Maine: A Volunteer Regiment in the Civil War* (1957; paperback: Dayton, Ohio, 1983); Willard M. Wallace, *Soul of the Lion: A Biography of General Joshua L. Chamberlain* (1960; paperback: Gettysburg, 1991); Alice Rains Trulock, *In the Hands of Providence: Joshua L. Chamberlain and the American Civil War* (Chapel Hill, 1992). The best work on the battle remains Edwin B. Coddington, *The Gettysburg Campaign: A Study in Command* (New York, 1968). A new synthesis is much needed. See also Boritt, ed., *The Gettysburg Nobody Knows*, especially Glenn LaFantasie, "Joshua Chamberlain and the American Dream." The best work on day two, with Chamberlain placed in context, is Harry W. Pfanz, *Gettysburg: The Second Day* (Chapel Hill, 1987).

10. George R. Stewart, *Pickett's Charge: A Microhistory of the Final Attack on Gettysburg, July 3, 1863* (Cambridge, Mass., 1959), remains the best work on the subject. See also Kathleen R. Georg and John W. Busey, *Nothing but Glory: Pickett's Division at Gettysburg* (Highstown, N.J., 1987); and Gary W. Gallagher, *The Third Day at Gettysburg and Beyond* (Chapel Hill, 1994). A new history is needed.

11. On this subject see Gabor S. Boritt, "'Unfinished Work': Lincoln, Meade, and Gettysburg," in Boritt, ed., *Lincoln's Generals* (New York, 1994), 79–120; and A. Wilson Greene, "From Gettysburg to Falling Waters," in Gallagher, ed., *The Third Day at Gettysburg*, 161–201.

12. William Faulkner, *Intruder in the Dust*; William E. Gladstone quoted in Howard Jones, *Union in Peril: The Crisis over British Intervention*

in the Civil War (Chapel Hill, 1992), 182; Roy P. Basler, ed., Marion Dolores Pratt and Lloyd A. Dunlap, assist. eds., *The Collected Works of Abraham Lincoln*, 9 vols. (New Brunswick, 1953–55), 8:333.

13. Most blacks who served at Gettysburg were enslaved. However, we know almost nothing about these Confederates. The subject badly needs scholarly scrutiny.

14. In its depth and quantity, the Lincoln literature, like that on Gettysburg, is unmatched in American historical writing. David Herbert Donald, *Lincoln* (New York, 1995), will become the standard biography. William Hanchett, *Out of the Wilderness: The Life of Abraham Lincoln* (Urbana, Ill., 1994), provides a good, quick introduction. The finest brief overview is Mark E. Neely, Jr., *The Last Best Hope of Earth: Abraham Lincoln and the Promise of America* (Cambridge, Mass., 1993).

15. Basler, ed., *The Collected Works of Lincoln*, 3:316. See also Gabor S. Boritt, "'And the War Came'? Lincoln and the Question of Individual Responsibility," in Boritt, ed., *Why the Civil War Came* (New York, 1996).

16. Lincoln's actual words were these: "At what point ["whence," above is a reasonable substitute] shall we expect the approach of danger? . . . Shall we expect some transatlantic military giant, to step the Ocean, and crush us at a blow? Never! All the armies of Europe, Asia and Africa . . . could not by force, take a drink from the Ohio, or make a track on the Blue Ridge, in a trial of a thousand years." The final two sentences are not reproduced here since they are quoted accurately. Ibid., 1:109. I made no systematic check of the accuracy of quotations, but found some similar problems elsewhere.

17. Robert R.S. Gutman, *John Wilkes Booth Himself* (Dover, Mass., 1979), and Robert Gutman to Boritt, 1994.

18. Waterston was willing but, unlike Gerald Guiterrez at Lincoln Center, the Burns brothers were not. Sam Waterston to Gabor Boritt, January 4, 1995.

6. Ken Burns and the Romance of Reunion

Thanks to Lawrence Goldman, of St. Peter's College, Oxford, and Lynn Garafola, for penetrating comments on an earlier draft of this essay.

1. *Los Angeles Times*, April 3, 1990; Howells is quoted in David W. Blight, "'What Will Peace Among the Whites Bring?': Reunion and Race in the Struggle over the Memory of the Civil War in American Culture," *Massachusetts Review*, 34 (Autumn, 1993): 394–95.

2. Blight, "'Peace Among the Whites,'" 394.

3. For the history of Reconstruction, see Eric Foner, *Reconstruction: America's Unfinished Revolution: 1863–1877* (New York, 1988).

4.   Benedict Anderson, *Imagined Communities: Reflections on the Origin and Spread of Nationalism* (rev. ed.: London, 1991).

5.   Blight, "'Peace Among the Whites,'" 396.

6.   Two excellent recent studies explore the process of reunion from this vantage point: Stuart McConnell, *Glorious Contentment: The Grand Army of the Republic, 1865–1900* (Chapel Hill, 1992), and Nina Silber, *The Romance of Reunion: Northerners and the South, 1865–1900* (Chapel Hill, 1993). These works appeared after the completion of the television series, but the point about selective memory and invented traditions was readily available in earlier works, such as Eric Hobsbawm and Terrence Ranger, eds., *The Invention of Tradition* (Cambridge, Eng., 1983).

7.   W.E.B. DuBois, *Black Reconstruction in America* (New York, 1935).

8.   Geoffrey C. Ward, et al., *The Civil War: An Illustrated History* (New York, 1991), 273.

9.   Roy F. Basler, ed., *The Collected Works of Abraham Lincoln* (9 vols.: New Brunswick, N.J., 1953–55), VII: 301–2.

About the Authors

Robert Brent Toplin, Professor of History at the University of North Carolina at Wilmington, received his Ph.D. at Rutgers University. He is the editor of film reviews for the *Journal of American History* and the editor of *Hollywood as Mirror: Changing Attitudes Toward "Outsiders" and "Enemies" in American Movies* (1993). Professor Toplin is also author of *History By Hollywood: The Use and Abuse of the American Past* (1996). His earlier books include *The Abolition of Slavery* (1972), *Freedom and Prejudice: The Legacy of Slavery in the United States and Brazil* (1982), and an edited work, *Slavery and Race Relations in Latin America* (1974). Toplin has created historical dramas that appeared nationally on PBS Television, including *Denmark Vesey's Rebellion* (1982), *Solomon Northrup's Odyssey* (1984), *Charlotte Forten's Mission* (1985), and *Lincoln and the War Within* (1992). The films about Solomon Northup and Charlotte Forten also appeared on The Disney Channel.

C. Vann Woodward, Professor Emeritus at Yale University, received his Ph.D. from the University of North Carolina at Chapel Hill. He is the author of *Tom Watson: Agrarian Rebel* (1938), *Reunion and Reaction: The Compromise of 1877 and the End of Reconstruction* (1951), *Origins of the New South: 1877–1913* (1951), *The Strange Career of Jim Crow* (1955), *The Burden of Southern History* (1960), *American Counterpoint: Slavery and Reconstruction in the North-South Dialogue* (1971), *Think-*

ing Back: The Perils of Writing History (1986), *The Future of the Past* (1988), and *The Old World's New World* (1991).

Gary W. Gallagher, Professor of History at the Pennsylvania State University, received his Ph.D. from the University of Texas. His books include *The First Day at Gettysburg: Essays on Confederate and Union Leadership* (1992) and *The Second Day at Gettysburg: Essays on Confederate and Union Leadership* (1993), and he is the editor of *Antietam: Essays on the 1862 Maryland Campaign* (1989), *Extracts of Letters of Major Bryan Grimes to His Wife: "Written in Active Service in the Army of Northern Virginia"* (1986), *Fighting for the Confederacy: The Personal Recollections of General Edward Porter Alexander* (1989), *Struggle for Shenandoah: Essays on the 1964 Valley Campaign* (1991), and *The Third Day at Gettysburg and Beyond* (1994).

Catherine Clinton, formerly of Harvard University and now a writer for film and television, received her Ph.D. from Princeton University. She is author of *The Plantation Mistress: Woman's World in the Old South* (1984), *The Other Civil War: American Women in the Nineteenth Century* (1984), and *Tara Revisited: Women, War and the Plantation Legend*; editor of *Half Sisters of History: Southern Women and the American Past* (1994); and co-editor of *Divided Houses: Gender and the Civil War* (1992).

Gabor S. Boritt, Robert C. Fluhrer Professor of Civil War Studies and Director of the Civil War Institute at Gettysburg College, received his Ph.D. from Boston University. He is the author of *Lincoln and the Economics of the American Dream* (1978), *Changing the Lincoln Image* (1985), and *Lincoln's Generals* (1994), as well as co-author of *The Lincoln Image* (1984). He also edited *The Historian's Lincoln: Pseudohistory, Psychohistory and History* (1988), *Lincoln, the War President: The Gettysburg Lectures* (1992), and *Why the Confederacy Lost* (1993).

Eric Foner, Professor of History at Columbia University, received his Ph.D. from Columbia University. He is the author of *Free Soil, Free Labor, Free Men: The Ideology of the Republican Party Before the Civil War* (1970), *Tom Paine and the American Revolution* (1976), *Politics and Ideology in the Age of the Civil War* (1980), *Nothing But Freedom: Emancipation and Its Legacy* (1983), *Reconstruction: America's Unfinished Revolution, 1863–1877* (1989), *A Short History of Reconstruction* (1990), and *A House Divided: America in the Age of Lincoln* (1991).

Leon F. Litwack, Morrison Professor of History at the University of California at Berkeley, received his Ph.D. from the University of California at Berkeley. He is the author of *North of Slavery: The Negro in the Free*

States, 1790–1860 (1965) and *Been in the Storm So Long: The Aftermath of Slavery* (1979), the co-editor of *Reconstruction: An Anthology of Revisionist Writings* (1969), and editor of *The American Labor Movement* (1962). He also authored a film, *To Look for America* (1971).

Geoffrey C. Ward, an author and former editor at *American Heritage*, was the writer for Ken Burns's television series, *The Civil War*. Educated at Oberlin College, he is the author of *Lincoln's Thought and the Present* (1978), *Treasures of the Maharajas* (1983), *A First Class Temperament: The Emergence of Franklin D. Roosevelt* (1990), *American Originals: The Private Worlds of Some Singular Men and Women* (1991), *Before the Trumpet: The Young Franklin Roosevelt* (1994), and *Civil War* (1994). Ward co-wrote *The Civil War* (1990) and *Baseball: An Illustrated History* (1994). He has also served as a scriptwriter for television programs, including *The Shakers: Hands to Work, Hearts to God* (1984), *Lindbergh* (1990), *Nixon* (1990), *The Kennedys* (1992), *George Marshall and the American Century* (1993), and *Baseball* (1994).

Ken Burns, filmmaker and founder of Florentine Films, received his undergraduate degree from Hampshire College. His documentary films include *The Brooklyn Bridge* (1981), *The Shakers: Hands to Work, Hearts to God* (1984), *Huey Long* (1985), *The Statue of Liberty* (1985), *Thomas Hart Benton* (1988), *The Congress* (1988), *The Civil War* (1990), *Empire of the Air* (1992), and *Baseball* (1994). Burns is co-author of *The Civil War* (1990) and *Baseball: An Illustrated History* (1994).